What release from legali
struggle with daily time v
all of us live life to a daily
according to our own individual life rhythms offers grace instead
of guilt, freedom instead of failure. Thank you, Gwen. The truths in
this book will transform!

—Jean E. Syswerda, author, editor, former associate
publisher of Zondervan Bibles, coauthor of bestselling
Women of the Bible and *NIrV Read with Me Bible*

A brilliant work, *Unforced Rhythms* calls us to be intimate with
God without feeling the guilt, shame, or fear of not fitting into
others' patterns or standards. Gwen writes simply, yet profoundly.
Read it and reap!

—Edward David, public relations director, OM Ships International

Most of us who claim to be followers of Christ want to say we are
great at devotions, while, in fact, we may do them out of guilt.
We ask ourselves—are they long enough, deep enough, good
enough? Gwen has done it! She helps us see God isn't looking
for us to put an "X" in a box each day. He desires that we walk in
rhythm with him and for each of us that looks different. Are you
ready to spend time with God in freedom? If so, read this honest,
life-changing book!

—Dan Seaborn, founder of Winning at Home, Inc.

As Christian leaders, we face a pretty stern set of expectations
to have early morning devotions—piled on top of early morning
workouts and arrivals to the office before everyone else, and
other demands of a secular world that lives without the burden
of spiritual disciplines. It's not surprising so many feel defeated.
Gwen gives us hope in the face of defeat. God is actually greater
than our self-imposed disciplinary patterns. He can fill and
establish a relationship with anyone, regardless of their natural
rhythm. Perhaps it's time for a new kind of spiritual awakening—
and maybe it doesn't have to happen early every morning!

—Mike Hilson, pastor of New Life Wesleyan Church, La Plata, Maryland

There are books where the "aha" not only invigorates the mind
but breathes life into the soul. Gwen's insights into the rhythms
of spiritual formation increase our capacity to keep in step with
the Spirit. No doubt the freedom and freshness that result will
bring you to the same conclusions as me—this book is well worth
reading.

—Wayne Schmidt, general superintendent of The Wesleyan Church

As someone with a similar faith journey as Gwen, this refreshing look at spiritual formation—disciplines—and moving from checklists to personal rhythms, was a delight to read and absorb! I deeply appreciate her redefinition of the goal of spiritual formation as "knowing and loving God for the sake of others," with the piercing words that "a soul that does not love is not at rest." I'd recommend this to anyone exploring the radical claims of Christ, particularly those who have been in the church for a longer season or who are serving others through ministry.

—Amy Lynn Kelley, executive director of HOPE missions of new**hope** church and founder of the Street Hope Foundation

What a breath of fresh air! Gwen's brave vulnerability kicks open the door of permission for the rest of us to simply *be* with God. She beautifully articulates the freedom we long for but chide ourselves for desiring. *Unforced Rhythms* is water for the thirsty soul who is trying to achieve rather than receive God's immeasurable grace. Wish I'd had this book in my hands years ago!

—Heather Semple, lead pastor, Red Cedar Church, Rice Lake, Wisconsin

Gwen helps us think carefully about spiritual practices that deeply impact our relationship with God and the motivations behind those practices. I believe readers will be challenged to find more natural ways of living in the presence of God and letting the Lord guide the patterns, habits, and rhythms that will cause our relationship with him to flourish.

—Verne Ward III, Nazarene Global Mission director

This book is liberating! I have learned some important things about myself and how God uniquely designed me. Gwen shares personal insights with honesty and humility, touching my heart and releasing my walk with God in a more authentic way that feels natural and guilt-free.

—Troy Beer, Australian National Church growth leader and senior pastor of Axis Church, Queensland, Australia

Unforced Rhythms is a spiritual Emancipation Proclamation for duty-bound Christians who feel they can never measure up when it comes to pleasing God. In this refreshing book, my friend Gwen Jackson shares her joyful discovery of "just living" in the "unforced rhythms of grace."

—Mark O. Wilson, author and assistant professor of discipleship, multiplication and renewal, Southern Wesleyan University

UNFORCED
RHYTHMS

why daily devotions
aren't for all of us

Gwen Jackson

wphstore.com
Indianapolis, Indiana

Library of Congress Cataloging-in-Publication Data

Jackson, Gwen, author.
Unforced rhythms : why daily devotions aren't for all of us / Gwen
    Jackson.
Indianapolis, Indiana : Wesleyan Publishing House, [2017] |
    Includes bibliographical references. |
LCCN 2017030448 (print) | LCCN 2017036809 (ebook) | ISBN
    9781632572158 (e-book) | ISBN 9781632572141 (pbk.) | ISBN
    9781632572158 (ebook)
LCSH: Spirituality--Christianity. | Devotional exercises. |
    Spiritual life--Christianity.
LCC BV4501.3 (ebook) | LCC BV4501.3 .J3263 2017 (print) | DDC
    248.3--dc23
LC record available at https://lccn.loc.gov/2017030448

CONTENTS

FOREWORD

To evangelicals, the practice of "daily devotions" has become a sacrament. More than that, for many, this ritual of getting up early, reading the Bible, and praying has become the prime sacrament, even edging out the Lord's Supper. Ask Christians for the single greatest secret of a successful Christian life, and most will answer, "morning devotions."

In this book, Gwen Jackson tackles the highly sensitive subject of how moderns have turned daily devotions into a required practice of the devoted life. It has become almost an idol to some. Any practice can become an idol when the method is worshiped more than God. Moses set up a pole to cure people from snakebites in the wilderness as a wonderful means of healing and grace. Yet later, Israel turned to worshiping the pole itself. The means of grace got more attention than God. This is what some Christians have done with daily devotions.

Have you felt this pressure to fit into the daily devotions mold, even though your life runs on a different rhythm? Many of us have been told the really elite Christians also maintain *a prayer list*, and they spend time *journaling* as well. Some preachers promised us that, after an hour—or two, or three—of this "time alone with God," we would "come down from the mountain" with faces aglow from having spent time with Jesus before breakfast each day.

This is what we've been urged to practice: piety as a solitary practice, preferably in the morning, on a twenty-four-hour cycle. When someone turns their back on God and falls into grave sin, we warn each other, "Better keep up on your devotions, or you could fall too." Face it, you've probably never heard someone say, "Better keep taking communion or you, too, could fall like that?" In today's church, daily devotions have become the number one sacrament. This is the primary way we expect God to change us—even more so than attending church.

The author of this book does not diminish the importance of prayer or Bible reading. She deeply believes in and practices these disciplines. These practices, and more than a dozen others, have been honored among Christians for more than a thousand years. What this author does challenge, however, is the notion that prayer and reading on a twenty-four-hour cycle—the *daily* and *morning* part of daily morning devotions—should be a requirement for all people. She urges us to make room for other rhythms of personal spiritual practice.

This must have been a tough book to write. Who wants to appear to be disassembling what has become a sacramental rite? Wouldn't the church be better if *more* people had daily devotions, not fewer? Yet Gwen does not discourage people who keep a daily regimen of prayer and Bible reading to stop. She merely offers encouragement to the many folks who live to the sound of a different life rhythm. She tells these folk that they don't have to squeeze into a rigid box of traditional, daily devotional practices. People with different rhythms can also draw closer to God.

Are your daily morning devotions flourishing? Great! The premise of this book is not dangerous to you. It won't talk you out of your morning ritual. What it will do is give you ideas to expand your practices to include other rhythms beyond daily ones. Even if you are a "very daily person," you already have some weekly rhythms: Saturdays, Sundays, hump days. And for sure you have annual rhythms like birthdays, vacations, back-to-school weeks, Christmas, Ash Wednesday, Lent, Easter, Pentecost, and Thanksgiving. This book is likely to inspire you to add some annual or seasonal practices to your spiritual rhythm. If your daily devotions are flourishing, read this book because it will expand your means of devotion.

Have you had trouble making devotions a daily routine? Perhaps you never felt quite right fitting into the glass slipper of daily morning devotions. Do you feel guilty? Are you embarrassed? Are you afraid you might be a substandard Christian? Maybe you've tried and failed so many times you've simply given up. For you, this book will be liberating! Here you will get to know one of the great saints of our age, an author who struggled just like you before discovering there is more than one way to draw close to God. You'll find alternative paths, based on other rhythms—unforced rhythms. You will be delighted to discover there is a size that fits you, *your* rhythm, *your* time of life, and *your* schedule. For you, this book will be absolutely liberating!

Or, are you a pastor or church leader? This book will help you develop a new vocabulary of devotion. It will prod you to stop elevating daily morning devotions as the best or even the only way to know God. It will draw you back to core practices like prayer and Bible reading instead of the package we've been putting these into. When we do, we will lead more church folks into greater devotion to God because they will have found the rhythm of life that works best for them. And that will be a great thing!

—Keith Drury

PREFACE

I might as well say it from the start. I don't do daily devotions. There. I said it. If you think that statement puts me on some slippery slope to spiritual death, it's probably best if you don't read on. On second thought, perhaps it would be best to keep reading. You'll find this book sheds light on other ways to spend time with God, giving grace to celebrate the uniqueness of others no matter how they choose to engage with him.

Some who read that first sentence probably felt immediate relief. If that was you, then read on, my friend; you're about to discover a life-giving, liberating perspective.

You'll discover not all believers fit into the same box when it comes to spiritual growth. And you'll realize that our life in Christ is measured (I hate to even use that word) by who we are and how that identity impacts others, not by when, where, or how we spend time with God.

I'd venture to say every genuine believer has a desire to know Christ and to grow in character, yet how we go about that growth can look very different from one person to the next. If we learn to live in the unforced rhythms of God's grace—rhythms both unique and natural to us—we will keep company with Jesus and find rest in his love. In this place of relationship, we find rhythm and rest. And, in this place, we are free to fully live and to genuinely love others.

Are you tired? Worn out? Burned out on religion? Come to me. Get away with me and you'll recover your life. I'll show you how to take a real rest. Walk with me and work with me—watch how I do it. Learn the unforced rhythms of grace. I won't lay anything heavy or ill-fitting on you. Keep company with me and you'll learn to live freely and lightly.

—Matthew 11:28–30

ACKNOWLEDGMENTS

I f it weren't for David Drury, I would have never known the liberating truth of life rhythms. It was the final freedom point that gave practicality in my search for what time with God could be, rather than what I thought it should be. When you wrote that two-page article, David, you wrote it for me. Thank you!

I'm quite sure there would be no book, if not for Christin Taylor. Her expertise in editing for a first-time author saved me in so many ways, perhaps the greatest being my own critical voice. Her encouragement and affirmation kept me going, even when she suggested that I rewrite whole chapters. Thanks for "paying it forward," Christin. I can't thank you enough!

From our first encounter on a university campus, my husband, Dennis, has been giving me the amazing gift of high belief. Especially at the onset of our relationship, his belief in me was far higher than what I could see in myself. And, so it is with this book. He's been calling me an "author" from the beginning stages of sloppy first drafts. Honey, thanks for speaking my love language!

To all my readers, I pray the message of freedom will ring true in your heart. May the unforced be with you!

INTRODUCTION

vulnerability,
the key to connection

I can't believe I'm telling you all this," Courtney said as she sat across the table from me. We had been sitting in a coffee shop in downtown Indianapolis for over an hour. My twenty-something daughter had connected the two of us. "Mom, would you be willing to meet with a friend of mine?"

It was the first time I had met Courtney, a mid-twenties young woman who was wearing jeans, a wool sweater, and ankle-high boots on that crisp, fall day. With a soft, patterned scarf layered around her neck, she had the look of rugged cuteness. Her pixie cut was perfect for her round face, her black hair matching equally dark eyes.

I listened to her story, the current life situation that had brought the two of us together. Three-plus hours later, we exchanged a hug and set up a time to meet again in the near future. Courtney and I met consistently for the next three years until she made a move to the West Coast. Ironically, Courtney must have sensed that I was writing about her because I received a text while writing this portion of the book: "Hey Gwen! You free to chat tomorrow or Saturday sometime?"

Connecting with people one-on-one is one of my favorite things to do. I love meeting people, hearing their stories, and getting to know them through those stories. Surface talk has its place, but going deeper, to the soul and spirit of a person, allows perspectives to change and understanding to take root. This is where I like to live. I love coming alongside others, wherever they might be on the journey of life. When I'm sitting across from someone, I listen with an ear to understand. My empathy and restorative nature (thanks, *Now, Discover Your Strengths*[1]) kick in big time, along with my desire to encourage and support with love and understanding.

If I can't sit across from a person due to distance, the next best thing is to connect through written communication. There was a day when I would actually write a letter on paper, seal it in an envelope, place a stamp on it, and pop it in the mailbox. Now delivery is expedited via email or social media. When I'm creating a message, seeing the face of the person to whom I'm writing makes the experience personal. I share from my own life. My vulnerability tells the other person they aren't alone. It gives them hope.

In her book *Daring Greatly*, Brené Brown, a researcher on shame and vulnerability, describes vulnerability as "the core, the heart, the center, of meaningful human experiences."[2] Without vulnerability, how does one relate with another? Vulnerability opens the heart for connection. It paves the way for open and meaningful relationships. Without it, how can I truly know you, and how can you truly know me? Within the pages of this book, you'll hear my heart. These chapters must be marked by vulnerability. Without it, it wouldn't be me writing. I can't pretend.

On my fortieth birthday, my husband invited four couples to join us for a relaxing and meaningful evening, honoring my request for a quiet and simple celebration. Without my knowledge, he had asked each person to write words of affirmation and be prepared to read them aloud to me. On that delightful evening, surrounded by friends in a cozy living room, words of love and acceptance tumbled into my heart, words that described who I was from those who knew me well. A common thread joined the words of all eight friends: real. sincere. authentic. genuine. Vulnerability produces this in me. I can't not be real.

I trust you'll hear my heart as you read, yet my vulnerability carries a risk. Part of me fears writing this book because I wonder what people will think of me. Will fellow believers gasp at the idea that my spiritual rhythm does not include a daily time with God?

I fear I'll be misunderstood.

I fear that others will think I'm judging those who have (and enjoy) daily devotions.

I fear some will remain in bondage to a ritualized way of doing things while others may take my words as a license to spend no time with God at all.

But what I fear most is you'll miss the point I hope to make: the goal of spiritual formation—Christ formed in us—is to know and love God for the sake of others.

Yet my courage and fear have met, so I am "daring greatly" by writing this book. It has taken courage to share my life, to share the things that have freed me to live in Christ through who I am. My relationship with Christ is a grace-filled journey—engaging with God through my unique life rhythm, finding my identity in him as his beloved child, and expressing his love to others through my personality, strengths, and gifts.

It has also been encouraging to find, after beginning to share these insights with others, that I am not alone. This means you're not alone either. The discovery that I'm not the only one who struggles with the expectations that have produced chronic defeat in my spiritual life has reassured me. That is what happens when we hear someone say, "Me, too." Shoulders relax when we begin to be real. Perfectionism and concern for what other people think melt away.

As I am writing, I am thinking of the faces of many in the world who struggle with spiritual expectations, forced disciplines, and the need to measure up. Such expectations—perhaps imposed by Western church culture or locked in by traditional values—often put a person of genuine faith on a path that feels like legalism, while yearning for intimacy with Christ apart from a formula or ritual. Some of you I have met, and others I know only through a shared understanding of this spiritual struggle.

I pray the words of this book may flow like a letter to a dear friend. I trust they will begin a dialogue not only between you and me but also between yourself and others, and that that dialogue will produce conversations filled with grace.

This book describes my journey away from the burdensome expectations—sometimes self-imposed—that drained the joy from my spiritual life and left me defeated, into the grace-filled spirituality that fits the rhythm of who God created me to be. It is part spiritual memoir, part guidebook. As I relate my story, you'll find plenty of help here for your own journey too.

The early chapters of this book describe various aspects of both the bondage I felt in living under unrealistic spiritual expectations and the discoveries I made that led me to freedom. This journey was not linear for me, and the story is not told in a linear fashion. Some chapters will feel circular, as if we are dealing once again with spiritual problems already faced and overcome. Those chapters simply deal with a different aspect or nuance of my struggle, examining the same problem from a fresh angle. There was no single aha moment that led to my freedom. It came after years of one small victory at a time, sometimes followed by lapses back into spiritual defeat.

As we begin this conversation, let me tell you what this book isn't about and then what it is about. It's not about throwing prayer and Bible reading out the window; it is about discovering a new perspective on living in relationship with God and others.

It's not about opposing spiritual practices. It is about understanding and appreciating the heart of those practices.

It's not about bashing those who have daily quiet times. If anything, I admire those who practice that discipline. Their consistency is something I strived to achieve for years. I celebrate their discipline! It is about doing away with self-imposed burdens, false expectations, chronic defeat, and perfectionism—the very things that keep us from truly living and loving in the name of Christ.

Part 1 of this book exposes four barriers to intimacy with God, opening the pathway to freedom. This book is about living an abundant life, as Jesus promised.

Part 2 brings us to the discoveries I made that led to my freedom to relate to God in a new way. Chapter 5 will demonstrate that the main thing in our spiritual lives is to "just live" for God, free from burdensome rituals and false guilt. And chapter 6 reveals that we can trade in our burdens—guilt, defeat, and shame—for the "burden" Jesus offers: love. Chapter 7 recounts my discovery of the concept of "life rhythms," the three different beats by which we may find ourselves navigating life—and our relationship with the Father.

Part 3 explores life rhythm in more detail. Chapters 8 through 11 describe the three rhythms and how to live by them. You'll find yourself leaning into one of them more than the others. I've illustrated each category with scenes borrowed from those I know intimately—my mom, my husband, and myself. And, you'll hear from real people who have found freedom to embrace their unique life rhythm as it relates to knowing God and doing life.

Part 4 focuses on the significance of spiritual formation. In chapter 12 you'll learn why we do what we do to be formed spiritually. In the final chapter, we'll talk about spiritual practices, though this is not an exhaustive treatment. Much has already been written on this subject. We will clarify why these practices exist—to assist us in spiritual formation. You'll come away with an increased desire to benefit from these time-honored practices.

This book is about understanding the rhythm of your life and allowing it to shape and form your intimacy with Christ.

It's about maturity for the sake of others.

It's about celebrating each other's differences.

It's about uniqueness.

It's about freedom.

It's about God's love and grace.

Pull up a chair. Let's have a cup of coffee or your favorite tea. It's good to meet you!

BARRIERS
TO INTIMACY
WITH GOD

part 1

1
OUGHT AND SHOULD

the barrier of self-imposed burdens

We might be functioning out of an inordinate sense
of "ought and should," burdened by unrealistic
expectations about what it means to be a good Christian.

—Ruth Haley Barton, *Sacred Rhythms*

$\mathcal{I}$ distinctly remember one winter afternoon in my favorite coffee shop in the city of Budapest. Even though it was a ten-minute walk plus a twenty-five-minute tram ride from the flat where we were living at the time, I found it worth the travel time. Good coffee, friendly baristas, and a variety of seating options drew me back repeatedly. Besides that, coffee shops inspire me. It could be the aroma of coffee that floats in the air or the ambient noise that drowns out some of my mental hum, but either way, coffee shops provide inspiration that can carry me for several hours at a time.

That day, I had settled into a comfy chair in the corner. With my computer in my lap, I sorted through email while sipping a vanilla latte. My eyes landed on a thread of messages from my prayer team, a select group of women who came alongside me in prayer throughout our time in Europe. I often asked how I could pray for them as well, and Erica, whom I had known for over twenty years, had responded with a concern about her spiritual growth. I first met Erica when she was dating Jon, who did a summer internship with my husband, Dennis, at a local church. After Jon's college graduation, Dennis had the privilege of performing Jon and Erica's wedding ceremony. That summer internship grew into a lifelong friendship.

In her email, Erica asked for prayer and guidance in dealing with her feelings of guilt when she didn't "daily find time for the Lord." She said she did best when she was part of a group in which there was accountability to do a lesson or study at home, but even then she felt like she was only "going through the motions." She also said she enjoyed connecting with God through music and reflective prayer but added, "I don't make time for this daily." Erica's frustration was not new. She wrote: "I have been a Christian for twenty-eight years, and I know what I 'should' be doing, but I struggle with making it real sometimes, and feeling connected with God during devotional time."

Erica desired to have intimacy with God but struggled to make her time with God meaningful on a daily basis. That was something I could relate to. In fact, the same tension had been brewing in me for years.

GROWING UP IN THE CHURCH

My parents took me to church from the time I was born. My mom's parents, Papa and Nana to me, helped care for babies in the church nursery, and it was there where I first began to learn of God. I can still visualize the preschool Sunday school class where I played on a wooden rocking boat that, when turned upside down, became steps to toddle up and over. Simple songs, often accompanied by hand motions, taught of God's love and care for me. Stories from the Bible were told with pictures and songs. The story I remember best was that of Zacchaeus. While making climbing motions, we sang of the "wee little man" who "climbed up in a sycamore tree" because "the Lord he wanted to see."

Luke tells us Zacchaeus was a short man and a chief among those in the Roman tax-collecting business (see Luke 19:1–10). His profession made him an affluent man, but it also carried a poor reputation. The general public considered tax collectors a disreputable bunch because of their dishonesty in overcharging people on their taxes. Crowds of people had gathered in Zacchaeus' hometown of Jericho, knowing that Jesus was coming through on his way to Jerusalem. Word about Jesus was out, and people were amazed at his miracles and authority.

Curiosity drew Zacchaeus to the crowded streets. Desperately trying to get a glimpse of Jesus, Zacchaeus decided to run farther down the road. He spied a sycamore-fig tree, climbed it, and waited for Jesus to pass by. Zacchaeus watched with eagerness as he parted the deep green leaves of the tree. Who was this man, Jesus? Maybe

Zacchaeus had gotten wind of Jesus' story of a tax collector who prayed with a humble heart, compared with an arrogant Pharisee (see Luke 18:9–14). Or perhaps Zacchaeus had heard of Jesus' conversation with a wealthy man who couldn't give up his riches in order to gain eternal life (vv. 18–23). No doubt perplexed and thrilled at the same time, Zacchaeus kept watching.

When Zacchaeus saw Jesus in the crowd, his eagerness turned to bewilderment. Jesus stopped right in front of the low-hanging limbs of the sycamore. The crowd stopped. Zacchaeus didn't know if he should duck behind the leaves or continue to gaze upon this man. Looking up into the branches, Jesus saw Zacchaeus peeking through. By now Zacchaeus' heart was pounding. Then he heard his name: "Zacchaeus." How did Jesus know his name? Jesus called out over the crowd's voices, "Zacchaeus, hurry down. Today is my day to be a guest in your home" (Luke 19:5–7).

As a child, I know I didn't think through all the implications of the story, but what a wonder it would have been for Zacchaeus to hear his own name called out by Jesus. Beyond that, Jesus was inviting himself to Zacchaeus' home! Flabbergasted, Zacchaeus scrambled down the tree and took Jesus home with him. That was the end of the Jesus parade. The crowd dispersed, just as astonished as Zacchaeus was, though some likely followed to see if Jesus was true to his words. Their astonishment was undoubtedly mixed with ridicule and displeasure at the thought that Jesus had invited himself to the home of a despised tax collector. Even so, that day transformed Zacchaeus' life.

Jesus called Zacchaeus by name, initiated a relationship with him, and then dined with him in the comfort and familiarity of Zacchaeus' own home. After meeting with Jesus face-to-face, Zacchaeus decided to make his wrongs right. He promised to give back four times the amount he had cheated people on their taxes, and he committed to giving half his wealth to the poor. It's an astounding story of redemption.

At the age of ten, I had my own life-changing experience. I wasn't sitting in a tree but in the same church where I'd learned of Zacchaeus. It was during a weeklong series of nightly services given by a visiting evangelist, not an unusual event for evangelical churches in the 1960s and '70s. Sunday school classes were canceled to accommodate an added Sunday service, and I sat with my fellow fifth graders on folding chairs in the overflow section, behind the main sanctuary. I don't remember who the preacher was or what he said that day, but I do remember how I felt when, at the end of his message, he invited anyone who desired to invite Jesus into his or her heart to come and kneel at the altar at the front of the church.

While the congregation sang "Amazing Grace," my heart began to pound and tears welled up in my eyes until they spilled over. The girl next to me looked curiously at me, seemingly unaffected by the message. But like Zacchaeus, desperate to see Jesus, I longed to have him in my life. And like Zacchaeus, I heard my name. Jesus was calling me, inviting me to let him into my heart's home.

Yet if it had been unlikely that Jesus would notice Zacchaeus sitting in that sycamore-fig tree, it was even more unlikely that I would have the courage to walk down the center aisle of the church to pray at the altar. As far as I could see, no one was moving, and I certainly wasn't bold enough to be the first. Then I felt a hand on my shoulder. I looked up to see my dad. He had been sitting several rows behind me and noticed my tears. "Do you want to go forward?" he asked.

I nodded my head "yes," and, hand in hand, we made our way to the altar. Together we kneeled. Others eventually knelt on either side of us, responding in faith to the message they had heard.

The sensitivity of my dad that day will forever hold a special place in my heart: my earthly father led me to my heavenly Father. Dad knelt with me as I prayed a prayer confessing my sins. Tears ran down both our faces as I thanked God for sending his Son, Jesus, to give his life for my sin so that I might have eternal life. With joy, I accepted Jesus' invitation to make himself at home in my heart. I remember immediately feeling clean inside. It's the only way I can explain it. Something had happened in me, and I knew it was because of Jesus. The next morning, I got on the school bus with a desire to tell others what had happened. Jesus lived in me, and I wanted to live for him.

Though I had lots of learning and growing to do, my commitment to live for Jesus was unwavering from that point on. The spiritual highlight of my teen years came the summer before my senior year of high school, when I attended Explo '72, a Campus Crusade for Christ event held in Dallas. Along with a crowd of over 80,000— mostly high school and college students—I sat in the packed Cotton Bowl stadium under the hot Texas sun. The atmosphere in the stadium was contagious and

AT THE
AGE OF TEN,
I HAD MY OWN
LIFE-CHANGING
EXPERIENCE.

exhilarating. Our young hearts wanted to grasp more of Jesus.

During one of the evening rallies, Bill Bright, the founder of Campus Crusade, gave a message on being filled with the Holy Spirit. That night I committed myself to follow Jesus more fully by surrendering my whole life to him. It was a sanctifying experience. I set myself apart for God, giving all that I knew of myself at that time to all that I knew of him. That became an ongoing growth point for me, because as I discover more things about myself—through life experience, through trials, and relationships—I am reminded that I am always in need of further transformation. The more I discover about God, whom I can never fully comprehend this side of heaven (see Rom. 11:33; 1 Cor. 13:10–13), the more I am in awe of his mercy, grace, and love for me.

A SPIRITUAL ANGST

As my walk with Jesus began to mature, I was eager to be everything God wanted me to be. To me, that meant following "the rules" for living the Christian life. Overall, the church conveyed there were essential practices that led to a believer's growth. New Christian follow-up material usually contained four key elements: read the Bible daily, pray daily, witness by sharing your faith, and attend church regularly. Over time, these four practices became the only things that mattered—rules to be followed. If I was consistent in each one, I was doing all the right things to become a mature believer.

Before long, a seed of guilt sprouted deep within my being. This guilt grew particularly when I didn't spend time with God on a daily basis. I had been told that having personal daily devotions was essential to my spiritual growth, so for years I tried to fit into that box the Christian world had shaped. This package came with concrete numbers. I heard them time and time again from Christian speakers at conferences, in Sunday morning messages, and in books: a half hour with God every day was good—though even fifteen minutes was better than nothing—but an hour of Bible reading and prayer was really good. Go beyond an hour and, well, that made you a saint.

My spiritual life had come to be defined by who I ought to be and what I should be doing, not by my initial love for Christ.

These numbers were usually paired with specific times of the day. If this "quiet time" was spent in the morning, before the day began, you were a super saint. Bedtime was another viable option. Since I was a night owl rather than a morning person, neither sounded appealing to me. As these expectations grew, they began to choke out the tender shoot of my relationship with Christ. Defeat and discouragement cropped up to replace the victory and encouragement I first had in my life with Christ. My spiritual life had come to be defined by who I ought to be and what I should be doing, not by my initial love for Christ.

Looking back on those days, it's no wonder I had internalized these false expectations. The Christian publishing industry mass produces books, journals, and daily devotionals that unintentionally propagate these artificial standards for what a mature devotional life looks like. By whatever name we call it—spiritual discipline, quiet time, time alone with God, daily devotions—this practice is believed to be an essential component of Christian growth. Yet while I desired to be in God's presence, the struggle to set aside time each day created angst. I was torn between my desire for more of God and my anxiety at trying to follow "the rules" for Christian growth.

Sadly, the only daily routine in my spiritual life was the burden I felt to have devotional time and the condemnation I experienced when I didn't. The finger of accusation pointed all day. Guilty! I felt it in a thousand ways. If the day went haywire, well, it was because I hadn't had my devotions. When I did get my devotions in for the day, I was frustrated that I didn't have more time. God became a check box on my spiritual to-do list. When I checked the box, I felt legalistic, and when I didn't, I felt guilty. I didn't want it to be this way, but I didn't know what to do about it. I was living the reality that my friend, Erica, described as "just going through the motions."

FREEDOM

Sitting in that coffee shop in Budapest, I felt all of those emotions flooding back. With great empathy, I responded to Erica's email and, perhaps for the first time, put into words the discoveries that had released me from the weight of those terrible words *ought* and *should* in my spiritual walk. After decades of spiritual angst over this matter, I could write to her from a place of freedom, a freedom that empowered me to connect with God and others naturally and authentically. This freedom came to me bit by bit, through a series of life experiences, a new understanding of Scripture, and an acceptance of my uniqueness, which gradually released me from the pressure to follow a formula or a set of rules.

The self-imposed or others-imposed expectations no longer hovered over me. Instead, I found the grace to engage with God through the uniqueness of who I am without striving to be someone I'm not. And sometimes that grace finds me sitting in a coffee shop somewhere in the world, encouraging a friend via email while I sip my vanilla latte. I'd like to think that you and I are sitting across from each other, engaging in conversation as we journey through this book. There's no doubt in my mind that you're going to find your heart lighter, your spirit freer, and your soul less weary by the time we reach the end.

PERSONAL REFLECTION

1. What's your story of salvation? Take time to write it out or share it with a friend.

2. Did you relate with Erica's struggle? If so, in what way?

3. In what ways are you thankful for your spiritual upbringing?

2

MEASURING UP

the barrier of false expectations

We are not given favor because of our performance as
Christians, but because of our placement in Christ.

—Graham Cooke, brilliantperspectives.com

Measuring up. That was a major theme during my
formative years. It all started in third grade when I couldn't
get my multiplication tables down. My teacher would
have me stay inside during recess to work on them. I'd sit
at my little metal desk with its wooden top and attached
chair and labor over multiplication problems while the other
kids were outside playing. I could handle my multiplication
tables up to the fives. But I'd panic from six on up, especially
at the eights and nines. My teacher would time me. How
fast could I finish the problems? I'd try my best, but the
pressure to perform rattled my concentration. The clock
was always against me.

Measuring up. It's the constant pressure to achieve.

Unfortunately, I had the same teacher in fourth grade, so the pressure to measure up continued the next year and my feelings of inadequacy set in even deeper. Then came fifth grade, the worst of all my years in grade school. Toward the end of fourth grade, students had started a petition to get one of the fifth-grade teachers removed from the school. You know it's bad when fourth graders call for a petition! Unfortunately, she was the wife of the principal, a kind and gentle man, so the petition failed. That left every up-and-coming fifth grader in dread of the coming year. Apprehension turned to reality on the last day of fourth grade, when classroom assignments for the following fall were posted outside each classroom.

I was assigned to the dreaded teacher in a mixed class of fifth and sixth graders. Any positive self-image that remained after I'd finished third and fourth grade would be lost, or so my nine-year-old mind thought.

I was missing the grace God offered me in his love, a love not based on my performance.

We've all dealt with the need to measure up at some point. We've experienced those moments when we feel incapable, inadequate, or left out. We encounter them in school, sports, band, and choir, and even at birthday parties. Some of us rise to the level of teacher's pet, and others don't. At recess, we line up and wait while the team captains make their picks. Nobody wants to be the last one chosen. Some seem to have all the popular friends, and others don't. Some are chosen as homecoming king or queen, and then there are the rest of us. Some don't even imagine such things; they seem unattainable.

Beginning in those grade-school years, the pressure to measure up to the expectations of others was a constant battle in my life. And that war spilled into my spiritual life. Even after experiencing the freedom of salvation at age ten, I continued to make recommitments to Christ based on the fear the last one hadn't been enough. While in my teen years, I questioned this pattern. But I was told that it was a sign of growth—that as I grew, I would make renewed commitments to God. Though there is truth in that, I wonder if the recommitments I made in my youth were driven less by a true need to rededicate my life to Christ than by self-imposed expectations and fears, and feelings that I did not measure up to God's expectations.

READ YOUR BIBLE, PRAY EVERY DAY

Expectations. What is expected of a Christian? By what measurements does one qualify as a growing Christian, besides attending church regularly? Here are the answers I had begun to internalize:

- I needed to read my Bible daily.
- Time alone is necessary for Christian growth.
- Daily devotions are a mark of Christian maturity.
- To be truly spiritual, I must get up early in the morning to spend time with Jesus.

- Every day, I should spend fifteen or thirty minutes in prayer. Two hours in the early morning would be ideal.

I remember singing this song in Sunday school as early as my preschool years:

Read your Bible, pray every day,
Pray every day, pray every day.
Read your Bible, pray every day,
And you'll grow, grow, grow.
And you'll grow, grow, grow.
And you'll grow, grow, grow.
Read your Bible, pray every day,
And you'll grow, grow, grow.

My Sunday school classmates and I would crouch down just before the chorus; then, as we sang the "grow" part several times over, we gradually rose up to a full standing posture to show our growth.

At some point, someone added another verse.

Neglect your Bible, forget to pray,
Forget to pray, forget to pray.
Neglect your Bible, forget to pray,
And you'll shrink, shrink, shrink.
And you'll shrink, shrink, shrink.
And you'll shrink, shrink, shrink.
Neglect your Bible, forget to pray,
And you'll shrink, shrink, shrink.

With this addition, we would begin the chorus standing tall, and gradually lower ourselves into a squatting position to show the effect of neglect and forgetfulness.

It was all well-meant, and there is truth in this little song. But for me, trying to incorporate the daily reality of the song into my life became a burden that tormented my faith for years.

Certainly my Sunday school teachers had no idea this song would bring angst and torment to my faith. They were simply communicating Bible reading and prayer were important elements to knowing God. Looking back, my compliant nature became consumed with the "every day." If I was to read my Bible and pray every day, then that's what I should do. But along the way, I was missing the grace God offered me in his love, a love not based on my performance. Jesus wasn't the one pressuring me to perform. The weight of performance came from my self-imposed expectations, from my desire to please my teachers (both in school and Sunday school), and my need to be validated before God and others.

It took years for me to realize that my self-worth wasn't dependent on my ability to perform. Once I recognized those thoughts as lies from the enemy of my soul, I could renounce them as such and begin to find freedom to live outside of a performance-based faith. The fact that Jesus loved me, believed in me, and was proud of me simply because I was his child, was a truth that began to transform my mind and heart.

PERSONAL REFLECTION

1. List what you believe are the marks of a growing believer. Do you consider these marks to be biblical, self-imposed, or others-imposed expectations?

2. How do you understand the terms *conviction* and *condemnation*? How do you see both, or either, playing out in your life?

3. When do you most sense God's presence in your life?

3

DAILY GRIND

the barrier of chronic defeat

Chronic (adj.): continuing or occurring again
and again for a long time
Defeat (n.): frustration by nullification
or by prevention of success

—Merriam-Webster Dictionary

*O*ne day years later, after getting married and raising four teenagers, I was dusting the bookshelves in our bedroom. I took note that an entire shelf was filled with journals dating over a twenty-year period. Over the years, putting my thoughts to paper has been a life-giving and beneficial practice; it helps me make sense out of life.

I scanned the journals, pulling out a few to note the date marked on the front cover. I selected one from ten years earlier. Cleaning was going to be put on hold for a while. Making myself comfortable on the carpet, I leaned against the bookshelf and began to turn the pages of my life. Rediscovering thoughts from a decade ago, I began to see a common theme penned at the outset of many entries.

It's been too long since I've written in here.

Ugh! So many days have passed since I've spent time with the Lord.

Why is this so hard?

I'm sorry, God.

Self-condemnation and guilt struck me all over again. Typical entries were a week or two apart, evidence of my lack of daily quiet time. What was with me? Why couldn't I be more consistent? How could I call myself a mature believer? At the time, I had been growing in Christ for well over thirty-five years. But something was wrong. I wasn't getting this Christian life with its spiritual practices. Disciplined, I was not.

That very term, *discipline*, placed a burden on me that I couldn't handle. I desired to have intimacy with Christ, but I refused to use the term *spiritual disciplines*. To me, it meant a daily time set aside for God, and I couldn't seem to get it together in that regard. So I just took the term out of my vocabulary.

The problem was that my definition of discipline—training people to follow a code of behavior by using guilt—didn't fit the kind of relationship I desired with Jesus. This God was nit-picky, exacting, and perfectionistic, just like my grade school teachers. He was never satisfied with what I did, and I lived in fear or dread based on my performance, my practice of daily devotions in particular. Part of me wanted to throw in the towel, not on my Christian faith but on spiritual disciplines—though I'm sure I even considered abandoning the Christian faith in moments of exasperation.

I do wonder if this very thing causes some people to jump ship on the faith. They're sinking in a sea of expectations, either self-imposed or required by others. In desperation, do some abandon their relationship with God?

In one season of my life, I took an informal survey asking when people spent time with God—what time of day they devoted time to him and how that worked for them. I was desperately trying to figure it out, this devotional life. After searching the Scriptures, I found not one place where a devotional life was mentioned. Certainly, Scripture points to occasions when Jesus spent time seeking his Father in prayer. Jesus "often withdrew to the wilderness for prayer" (Luke 5:16 NLT). He went to the mountains and spent the night in prayer before choosing the twelve disciples (see Luke 6:12–13). He was in prayer the night of his arrest (see Mark 14:32–35). He prayed over people in need of healing. He prayed before important decisions. He prayed for the disciples and future believers (see John 17), and he continues to pray for us (see Rom. 8:34). There's no doubt that Jesus prayed; I just don't find evidence of a regular daily time in prayer. At the disciples' request, Jesus gave a brief example of how to pray and taught the effectiveness of persistent prayer. What Jesus models for us is the love and consistency he had in relationship with his Father.

Before I go on, perhaps I should define the term *devotional life*. To most Christians, that term brings to mind a daily, scheduled time designated for God in prayer and Bible reading. Generally, that time is scheduled in the morning.

WHAT JESUS MODELS FOR US IS THE **LOVE** AND **CONSISTENCY** HE HAD IN **RELATIONSHIP** WITH HIS FATHER.

That was another factor in my guilt. I'm not a morning person. For me, devotions had become a measuring stick for the Christian faith. That they occur daily seemed important, otherwise I was letting my spiritual life slide, which was a hindrance to my spiritual growth. It was just like the song said—

Read your Bible, pray every day,
and you'll grow, grow, grow.
Neglect your Bible, forget to pray,
and you'll shrink, shrink, shrink.

THE DEVOTIONAL LIFE

In his book *The Prayer Life*, Andrew Murray tells of a time in 1898 when two members of the presbytery in New York attended a conference that focused on a deeper spiritual life. They returned to their presbytery hoping to bring about a revival among their fellow ministers. In the first meeting called to this end, the chairman asked the question: "Brethren, let us today make confession before God and each other. It will do us good. Will everyone who spends half an hour every day with God in connection with his work hold up a hand?" One hand went up. Then, "all who thus spend fifteen minutes hold up a hand." Not even half the hands were raised. The chairman then asked who spent five minutes with God. This time all hands went up. One man confessed afterward he wasn't sure if he spent even five minutes in prayer every day.[1]

I certainly have benefited from Andrew Murray's books, especially *Abide in Christ,* a thirty-one-day devotional, but I can assure you I didn't read it in thirty-one days. His writings on the power of prayer have stirred me to pray with confidence. I share his story here because I believe it demonstrates how *daily* time with God became a measuring stick for spiritual growth.

There are thousands of daily devotional books—daily devotions for kids, for couples, for teens, for men, for women. Google the words *daily devotionals,* and you'll get pages upon pages of results. Certainly, the daily devotional has made its mark on the Christian world. But I wonder if it has also put some of us in angst about our spirituality.

The United Methodist Church first published *The Upper Room* in 1935, a well-known daily devotional that is still around today. Another little magazine that many long-time believers will know is *Our Daily Bread*, produced and published by Our Daily Bread Ministries in Grand Rapids, Michigan. The first publication of this little booklet appeared in April 1956. I can remember my mom reading it at bedtime while waiting for my dad to come in from his nightly rounds on the farm. Now in her eighties, Mom still sits in her bed reading a daily devotional before she scoots under the covers.

I'm not a morning person. For me, devotions had become a measuring stick for the Christian faith.

While attending a Christian conference in the early 1990s, I heard a speaker promoting her book on daily prayer with a companion journal. Every time I heard someone's story on connecting daily with God through devotions, feelings of discouragement set in.

Sitting there in my bedroom, reviewing my old journal, I formed a diagnosis for the condition expressed in my entries: chronic defeat. Trying to live out my spiritual life in the box marked *daily* was more frustrating than encouraging, more guilt-inducing than joy-producing, and more a duty than a delight. Notice I didn't say that my relationship with God was frustrating, guilt-inducing, and dutiful. I loved God with all my heart and enjoyed spending time in the Word and in prayer, but trying to live within the confines of a daily practice produced a huge pressure that clouded what should have been a delight.

PERSONAL REFLECTION

1. What feeling does the term *spiritual disciplines* evoke in you?

2. What spiritual practices are you currently engaged in? Why?

3. Describe your current practice of "time with God."

4
TWO TRAILS

the barrier of perfectionism

Two roads diverged in a yellow wood,
And sorry I could not travel both
And be one traveler, long I stood
And looked down one as far as I could
To where it bent in the undergrowth.

—Robert Frost, "The Road Not Taken"

Yosemite National Park is one of my favorite places. Even after frequent travels to numerous countries, my husband, Dennis, and I still think Yosemite is one of the most beautiful places in the world. And though we don't get to do it as often as we would like, hiking is one of our favorite pastimes. We've been to Yosemite three times together, and Dennis more than that. He took each of our four children on a high school senior trip. Each one could choose where they wanted to go in the continental United States. Three of our four children chose Yosemite, and the other chose a road trip to Boston, preferring city life and shopping to mountains and hiking. Years later, when our adult children and their spouses had scattered across the United States and the world, Yosemite became a gathering spot for a family vacation. Even now as I write about it, I have a longing to be there, to take in the fresh mountain air, and to be surrounded by the beauty of Yosemite Valley—ponderosa pines, granite cliffs, and the sound of Lower Yosemite Falls in the distance.

Half Dome, the park's iconic granite formation, is visible from several points in the valley. The natural granite monument, aptly named, rises almost five thousand feet above the valley floor creating a sight that always leaves me in awe. I wanted to conquer the challenge of hiking Half Dome while I was physically able. During that vacation, several family members, including my husband, took on the challenge. However, I opted to stay back with two of our daughters at a fork in the trail and wait for the Half Dome crew to return on their descent.

Eight years later, it was my turn to make the Half Dome trek. Dennis and I began our hike before the sun came up, which was necessary in order to finish the hike in one day. The "insanity factor" on this hike is nine out of ten—ten being intense in mental challenge, elevation gain, and treacherous footing—with an average hiking time of ten to fourteen hours. Believe me, halfway up the tricky, gravel-coated steps of the subdome, I began to question my sanity. I kept my eyes on the rock-hewn steps for the full five-hundred-foot climb. With nothing to grab hold of or hang on to, I was envisioning my not-so-timely death, all the while dreading the fact that going to the top meant having to come back down.

At several points along the way, we stopped to make a brief video of the journey for our kids. We stood on a footbridge to take the first video. The Merced River flowed madly below us, and the sound of Vernal Falls roared ahead of us. From there we started our ascent along the river below the falls on what is commonly known as the Mist Trail. At the base of the falls, the force of the current creates a mist (and sometimes a rainbow), producing wet and slippery trail conditions up to the top of Vernal Falls, especially in the spring when the river is flowing full force with runoff from the snow-covered mountains. Wearing our rain gear, we made the thousand-foot climb, carefully treading the six-hundred-plus stone steps to the top of the falls. Taking a short break, we laid out our wet gear to dry on the smooth granite rock. With the roar of Vernal Falls just yards away, Dennis gave a thumbs-up in our second video, but we reminded ourselves, "We still have a long way to go."

From there, we continued the one-and-a-half-mile ascent to Nevada Falls. Just over two hours into this section of the trail, we reached the top of the falls, where the river rushed over a 594-foot granite cliff. This scene called for the third video. With the thunder of the falls behind us, I shouted with spunk and enthusiasm about how we'd made the trek up the steep, rocky switchbacks from Vernal Falls in good time. We were feeling pretty good about ourselves. We were keeping up with some twentysomethings from Europe, which gave us a little pride. We had an air about us, one of confidence, bravery, and resolve.

Yet with each video, our voices lost a bit of the grit we'd started with. It took every ounce of energy I had to make the final four-hundred-foot ascent of the dome. Pulling on our work gloves, we gripped the cable, mustered our courage, and began the climb up the forty-five-degree slope of smooth granite rock. Step by step, pull by pull, we made it up to the top. The view from five thousand feet was majestic, but I was tired. I knew we had to hike back down over those steep, rocky steps on the subbase. I found myself eager to get to level ground.

I had trusted God to be my salvation, my Savior, but I eventually turned that trust into pleasing.

By the time we shot the last video, back to the place where we'd started our ascent on the footbridge, it was dusk and Dennis' voice trailed off, saying something about hoping the pizza place near our camping area would still be open. I knew if I made it to the top it would be rewarding to be able to say I did it—and I did it! After fifteen hours of hiking, we reached the camp with aching legs and the pride that comes from doing what you've set out to accomplish. Later that night, after pizza, we crawled into bed with muscles so sore it hurt to move.

A MATTER OF PERSPECTIVE

In retrospect, I can see that my hike up Half Dome was more about me—what I accomplished, what I could do, how I performed—than about the greater reality of the majestic mountains. That illustrates how some of us live the Christian life. It's more about our performance than about God.

Several years ago, while reading a book titled *True-Faced*, I found myself completely identifying with an analogy the authors used. They describe two roads—we'll call them two hiking trails—that determine how we think, live, and relate with God and others. We are faced with a choice between the two trails: grace and works. The trail you choose makes a big difference in your spiritual life.[1]

As you would find in Yosemite, these spiritual trails are clearly marked with signposts, giving hikers a sense of direction and destination. Imagine yourself coming to a fork in the trail. Often, such a fork comes in the early days of one's faith in Christ. The signpost before you carries two signs, pointing in different directions. One is marked "Pleasing God," and the other, "Trusting God."

The trail of Pleasing God focuses on self-effort, and though the hikers desire a strong and solid relationship with God, they become caught up in working hard on eliminating their sin and improving their relationship with God. On the trail of Pleasing God, hikers often use the catchphrase "being all that God wants me to be."

As I read *TrueFaced*, I could identify with the trail of Pleasing God. I had used that very catchphrase to describe myself in a bio. It was my life mission to help others be all that God wanted them to be. That sounded like a good, holy intention. I had trusted God to be my salvation, my Savior, but I eventually turned that trust into pleasing. I could trust him to save me from sin but not from myself. Somehow pleasing makes sense to us. Of course, we might say, I do trust God, but what I *really* want to do is please him. Pleasing is something I can do. It can be measured. I feel happy and satisfied when I can please someone. It's about me, my responsibility, my obligation or duty to someone.

The trail of Trusting God, on the other hand, seems abstract and passive. It's not so much about me as about another. It's about relying on someone else, believing in the strength, ability, and reliability of something or someone. For a good many years, I joined the hikers on the well-traveled trail of Pleasing God.

TRUSTING IS PLEASING

Scripture does speak of the importance of pleasing God. Paul encouraged the church of Ephesus, "Carefully determine what pleases the Lord" (Eph. 5:10 NLT). He wrote similarly to the believers in Colossae: "Then the way you live will always honor and please the Lord, and your lives will produce every kind of good fruit. All the while, you will grow as you learn to know God better and better" (Col. 1:10 NLT). And, he urges the believers of Thessalonica to "live in a way that pleases God" (1 Thess. 4:1 NLT).

In the eleventh chapter of Hebrews, commonly called the faith chapter, the writer highlights those who had great faith throughout the Old Testament. Enoch, one of these examples, simply disappeared from this earth. Amazingly, he went to heaven without dying because "he was known as a person who pleased God" (11:5 NLT). The writer of Hebrews followed this up with a point for the reader, "And it is impossible to please God without faith" (11:6 NLT).

Pleasing God is an element of the Christian faith. We are to be holy as he is holy. We are to bring him delight by the way we live. It brings him glory and honor when we live according to his ways. But the emphasis in the faith chapter is exactly that: faith. What pleased God was that these people in the so-called "Hall of Faith" *trusted* him. Pleasing God wasn't their highest aim. Knowing they could *trust* him with who they were in accordance with their faith was what mattered. There's a difference between "being all that God wants me to be," and "trusting God with who I am." The first is solo; the second is in companionship with God. The first is about striving and trying; the second is about confidence placed in God, not self. The second is about his transforming power, not our own efforts. It was their faith that mattered, and faith is trust.

That thought totally shifted my thinking. If my focus is only on pleasing God, then I have to ask: How can *I* please God? That question leads to a "try harder" mentality. What must I do? It leads me back to the pressure of measuring up. It brings condemnation and guilt when I can't do enough or do it right. It's striving to gain God's approval, to earn his favor, and to be validated by what I do.

The journey on the trail of Pleasing God leads to comparison, perfectionism, and discouragement. You get tripped up with false guilt, self-condemnation, and a distorted view of God. Yet you must keep going, keep striving, and keep following the rules because pleasing God is the goal.

I remember telling someone, "The Christian life is so hard!" No wonder that was my perspective. I was trying so hard to please God. It was like I was hiking up Half Dome, giving it all I had, competing with twentysomethings, and comparing myself to others on the trail, all to prove to myself (and others) that I could do it. I was determined to finish no matter what it took. But all in all, it was a grueling day that left my muscles crying for relief. Hiking Half Dome was fulfilling for one day, but that hard-driving effort to prove myself was not sustainable long term. It was tiring. Over time, it drained my spirit and soul. The same was true with trying to please God.

The trail of Trusting God covers a different territory. It's not that this trail has no challenges, but the difference is in the focus and perspective of the hiker. Several years ago, our kids gave us hiking poles for Christmas. Now we wouldn't think of hiking without them. The poles take the strain off our backs and give leverage for our knees. I like to think humility and grace are the hiking poles on the trail of Trusting God.

Humility is a willingness to be honest before God and others about who we really are. When we do that, our dependence on God increases, and that's a good thing. Until we face the reality of who we are and the reality of who God is, we live as if it's up to us. Without the vulnerability that comes from humility, we strive for perfection. We compare instead of relating. We sidestep the heart. We live in a false sense of reality.

Brené Brown defines the word *courage* in her TED Talk "The Power of Vulnerability." "Courage," she shares, "is to tell the story of who you are with your whole heart."[2] Vulnerability isn't a weakness. It's a strength. In her book *The Gifts of Imperfection* (a must-read for anyone who struggles with perfectionism), Brown describes what she calls "wholehearted living." This kind of living is a journey to "find the courage to live and love with our whole hearts."[3] That's courage. That's reality. That's the trail of Trusting God with who we are. I'd like to spiritualize that description of the wholehearted journey by adding that it is living and loving *God and others* with our whole hearts.

Grace is what God has for us when we face the reality of who we are and, with feeble knees, trust in him to be the one who empowers us to be strong and courageous as he transforms our lives. On the trail of Trusting God, the focus is on God, not me. I do not hike my faith journey alone. God walks with me. He is trustworthy. When I am humbly aware of unhealthy, sinful habits, he offers his love, grace, and mercy. He enables me to live rightly and to love generously. My faith is not either/or; it's both/and. It's both God *and* me working together.

GOD'S PART, MY PART

My friend, Dina, who is awesome in the kitchen, uses bread making to illustrate how this relationship with God works. Typically, the ingredients for bread are flour, sugar, salt, perhaps butter, and almost always yeast. Warm water, at just the right temperature, is added to the dry ingredients to create dough. If the water is too hot, the yeast will die; too cool, and the yeast will not activate. The dough is kneaded and formed into a ball, then placed into a greased bowl and left in a warm place to rise.

Without yeast, there is no leavening factor. To leaven is to infuse, to permeate so as to transform something from one thing to another. The yeast is invisible, yet it must do its work to make the dough rise. Yeast takes a small, dense ball of dough and turns it into a light and airy mass doubling in size and often rising above the edge of the bowl. Once raised, a soft punch into the center of the raised dough lets the air out. Then the dough can be formed into the desired shape for the bread. Once more, the yeast is given time to do its work before the dough is popped into the oven. A half hour or so later, the dough comes out of the oven as a golden-brown, yummy loaf of bread.

Dina's description of bread making provides an illustration of the dual work of spiritual formation that I can wrap my head around. "Be energetic in your life of salvation," the apostle Paul wrote to the church of Philippi, "reverent and sensitive before God. That energy is *God's* energy, an energy deep within you, God himself willing and working at what will give him the most pleasure" (Phil. 2:12–13).

We give energy to our bread by making sure the right ingredients are available and mixed together for the end product. Then we knead and shape the dough, which is our work in the dough-making process. But only the yeast will provide the energy to actually transform the dough. The Holy Spirit does his part by "willing and working," permeating us with his power, love, and grace so that we are transformed into his likeness.

This is the trail of Trusting God. The journey is one of togetherness. The hiking is lighter and freer, because the focus is on God rather than on our efforts. As with the yeast, only God can make us new from the inside out. His invisible presence penetrates us in order to transform us from the old person to a new kind of person.

In *Mere Christianity*, C. S. Lewis claims that Christians are not merely improved but transformed. He holds to the thought that "mere improvement is not redemption. . . . God became man to turn creatures into sons: not simply to produce better men of the old kind but to produce a new kind of man."[4] We have not merely improved lives but lives made new.

Only God can make us new from the inside out.

Paul makes it clear that transformation is the business of the Father. "God has united you with Christ Jesus. For our benefit God made him to be wisdom itself. Christ made us right with God; he made us pure and holy, and he freed us from sin" (1 Cor. 1:30 NLT).

It is only through God's love and gift through Christ that we are made new. His Spirit alive in us empowers us to be transformed from the inside out. When—not if—we realize that we have missed the mark of living rightly, we have a gracious and compassionate God who forgives and doesn't hold that sin against us anymore. He is a loving Father, not cruel or mean or easily angered.

When I realized the difference between the two trails, I made a U-turn in my Christian journey, retracing my steps to arrive at the trail of Trusting God. When I switched trails, my focus changed. I was free to be who God says I am without the burden of striving for perfection in order to please him or earn his approval. I hiked empowered by the truth that I am already loved and accepted. I hiked knowing he is proud of me, his growing child. My journey became about maturity, not perfectionism. I simply need to trust in who he says he is: a God of love, mercy, and grace. It's his loving arm around me, extending mercy and grace when I fall or fail. He offers loving compassion, not the long, pointing finger of harsh condemnation (see Rom. 8:1). More of us need to get on the trail less traveled. I think we'll find more grace, mercy, and love for each other on the trail of Trusting God. It's time to change course.

NEVER GOING BACK

Getting to the top of Half Dome took a lot of effort, to be sure. Switchback climbs, the constant ascent, the rock-hewn steps of the subbase, and the final pull up the cables to the top of Half Dome were rewarding yet exhausting. Pain medicine hardly touched my aching muscles and joints. Even so, I can say I did it and brag about the pure determination it took to make it to the top. You better believe I made a photo book just to document that day! I was pleased with myself. It was strenuous, exhausting, demanding—but not the way I want to hike the journey of life.

In the third stanza of Robert Frost's poem, the hiker considers which trail to take.

And both that morning equally lay
In leaves no step had trodden black.
Oh, I kept the first for another day!
Yet knowing how way leads on to way,
I doubted if I should ever come back.[5]

The trail of Trusting God, my friends, has made all the difference in my Christian journey. The trail of Pleasing God is not one I wish to take. Knowing how trust leads to acceptance, freedom, and love, I'll stick to the new trail and use my hiking poles of humility and grace.

PERSONAL REFLECTION

1. Before reading this chapter, which trail would you have followed: Pleasing God or Trusting God? Why?

2. Is there a recurring theme of condemnation in your spiritual practices? If so, how do you think God views that area of your life? See Romans 8:1.

3. How does trusting God, rather than pleasing God, change your perspective on your life right now?

DISCOVERIES
THAT BRING
FREEDOM

part 2

5

JUST LIVE

discovering what matters most

For when I tried to keep the law, it condemned me.
So I died to the law—I stopped trying to meet all
its requirements—so that I might live for GOD.

—Galatians 2:19 NLT

Though I had discovered the difference between pleasing God and trusting him, I still didn't have an answer for my angst about daily devotions. One day I was kneeling near the living room chair in our home, asking God to help me understand why I was in such turmoil over following what I believed were the marks of a Christian. In desperation I cried out, "Lord, I don't know what to do about this thing called devotions!" I let out a big sigh. At that moment, I heard two simple words: "Just live."

Did I hear that right? Just live? Was that you, Lord? What? Really? I'm to "just live"?

At first I wondered if it had been my voice. But, no, I wouldn't have come up with those words on my own. There was no doubt in my mind they were the voice of God's Spirit.

I stood up, amazed that God had answered just like that, and amazed at the simple yet profound words that God had just spoken. "That's it," I said out loud. "These words are for me. 'Just live.'" I let out another big sigh, this time not from desperation but relief.

I desired intimacy with Christ yet felt the constant burden of not measuring up, wondering if I had done enough. Had I read my Bible enough? Did I pray enough? Did I fast enough? Did I serve enough? Did I attend enough classes at church? I'm not claiming that any of these activities are wrong. By no means! They are all important elements of Christian growth. But I had felt torn between checking off a spiritual to-do list and developing a deep relationship with Christ. "Just live" was exactly what I needed to hear that day. His words were not condemning or judgmental but full of grace and freedom.

Not long after that, I was reading the book of Galatians, solely because I knew it had everything to do with grace. I knew that I wasn't being gracious to myself, much less receiving God's grace. Paul urged the churches of Galatia to be gracious to the non-Jews who had received the good news of Jesus. Paul also reamed out Peter, who was fluctuating between rules and grace depending who was present, Jews or Gentiles (see Gal. 2:11–14). Paul said that what really counts is "faith expressing itself in love" (5:6 NLT) and a changed life (6:15). My heart sprang to life when I read in Galatians, in essence, the words I heard that day by the living room chair. Paul wrote he was no longer trying to meet all the requirements of the law, "so that [he] *might live for God*" (2:19–21 NLT, emphasis added). Paul gave words to the dilemma I felt. Condemnation was a constant with daily devotions, or my lack of them. For me, daily devotions felt like law. I was thrilled to discover this freedom in the words "just live," but I was totally unprepared for the reaction it would bring from others.

THE PHARISEE PROBLEM

One day after that encounter with the Word, I shared my "just live" story with someone. She shook her head and said that God wouldn't say something like that. He wouldn't tell me to just live. This woman never explained why she didn't agree, but I gathered she thought this philosophy was too simple. How does one measure "just live"? Yet I knew I had heard God's voice, and I knew it was true. To have it confirmed in his Word was a bonus. Sometimes Christians are too busy striving and pleasing rather than trusting and living. The writer of James explained it's important to have faith, but faith without action (living) is nothing. It's not either/or; it's both/and. Faith *and* action. Faith *and* living a life of love (see James 2:14–26).

Sadly, the world seems to have noticed that Christians are often more concerned with measuring up to some religious standard than with simply living authentic, Christlike lives. Type "Why are Christians . . ." in a Google search and you'll find out what the world thinks of us. The sentence will be completed by a number of words that I'd rather not be known for, including *negative, mean-spirited, intolerant, hypocritical, judgmental, hateful, stupid,* and *obnoxious.* Though these words certainly don't describe all Christians, this is the view many people have of the church. No wonder many millennials are tired, frustrated, and done with church. They're not seeing a difference between those who call themselves Christians and those who don't. They might even find their not-so-God-fearing friends have more of Jesus' character than those who call themselves Christian. "What difference does faith make?" they may ask. They may feel they have been put in a box. Do this, don't do that; stay away from this, stay clear of that. We seem to have defined the Christian life in terms of measuring up, of keeping up appearances, and of meeting an arbitrary standard of behavior rather than defining it in terms of loving God and others. We've become better known for what we're against than what we're for. This is the result of pleasing rather than trusting.

The Pharisees, religious leaders in Jesus' day, were a lot like this. Following the rules was important, but in the Gospels you'll find that if Jesus rebuked someone, it was nearly always the Pharisees. He called them "white-washed tombs," saying they were clean on the outside, but filthy on the inside (Matt. 23:27 NIV). The Pharisees were diligent in following the rules and regulations of the Jewish law. They crossed every t and dotted every i. They didn't miss a stroke. Their snobbish attitude brought con-demnation on anyone who did less. And they struck out at Jesus time and time again when he went outside the box of their rules—613 laws plus thousands more regulations.

Sabbath keeping was often the issue that resulted in their accusation.

One day Jesus and his disciples were walking through a grainfield. Maybe it was a shortcut to their destination, or maybe they wanted some grain to provide a little nourishment to carry them to the next meal. Either way, the disciples began to snack on heads of grain. However, this wasn't just any day. It was the Sabbath, and according to Jewish law, harvesting grain was prohibited on the Sabbath. Some Pharisees always seemed to be hanging around Jesus, like paparazzi in the modern day, and they witnessed this act of "breaking the law." They called Jesus out: "Look, why are they breaking the law by harvesting grain on the Sabbath?" (Mark 2:24 NLT).

Really? The disciples were harvesting? I grew up on a farm, and let me tell you, there's a difference between full-on harvesting and merely picking a few kernels to munch on. Jesus stood up for the disciples, responding with a rhetorical question. "Haven't you ever read in the Scriptures what David did when he and his companions were hungry?" (v. 25 NLT). Just in case they hadn't, Jesus went on to inform them that David, who was fleeing for his life at the time, went into the house of God and broke the law by eating the sacred bread that only priests could eat. David shared

"The Sabbath was made to meet the needs of people, and not people to meet the requirements of the Sabbath."

the bread with his companions. Jesus followed up this history lesson by announcing a new reality. "The Sabbath was made to meet the needs of people, and not people to meet the requirements of the Sabbath" (v. 27). Human need trumped the rules and regulations of the Pharisees.

Yet the Pharisees persisted in their focus on keeping the rules. Not even witnessing a blind man seeing, a deaf person hearing, or a once-paralyzed man walking could shake their belief. Even after Jesus performed such miracles on the Sabbath, they continued to accuse him.

Matthew tells how Jesus healed a demon-possessed man who was blind and mute (see Matt. 12:22–37). Jesus set this man free and restored his health. Jesus gave him the opportunity to work again, to live again. Still, the Pharisees had the audacity to accuse Jesus of healing through the power of Satan. Once again, the Pharisees were more concerned with their rules and regulations than with loving people who desperately needed wholeness.

Jesus kept company with the wrong crowd, at least according to the Pharisees. He ate in the home of tax collectors, a despicable group who were known for cheating people on their taxes. I wonder what their conversations were like. I wish I could have heard the dialogue between Jesus and those that others despised. What did they talk about?

When you realize the general public held tax collectors in contempt, it's pretty crazy that Jesus called one to follow him. It began one day when Jesus was out in the community. He noticed Matthew doing his job, collecting taxes at his booth. Jesus walked up to him and said, "Follow me and be my disciple" (Matt. 9:9 NLT).

That night Matthew invited Jesus and his disciples for dinner, along with some of Matthew's tax collector friends. Of course, the paparazzi (better known as the Pharisees) showed up, caught Jesus in another compromising situation, and questioned his behavior. "Why does your teacher eat with such scum?" they asked his disciples (v. 11 NLT). Jesus, overhearing their question, shot back, "Who needs a doctor: the healthy or the sick? Go figure out what this Scripture means: 'I'm after mercy, not religion.' I'm here to invite outsiders, not coddle insiders" (Matt. 9:9–13). Jesus always had a way of silencing these self-righteous men.

WHAT REALLY COUNTS

What was Jesus doing in each of these stories? He was going outside the box of rules and regulations. He saw people as needing love and compassion for their problems, not deserving hatred and contempt for their failures.

Believers often want to know what counts, what matters. Is it how much time we spend in prayer, or when we pray? Is it how many times we read through the Bible? What about fasting? How often should we fast, and for how long? What about witnessing? Do I need to bring the gospel into every conversation? How much should we tithe? Do we tithe on gross income or net income? All these questions have to do with us. They're not about others.

Paul asked the believers of Galatia why they were reestablishing the old law when they had been saved by grace, which doesn't depend on performing certain rituals, observing specific dietary restrictions, and the like. Paul writes in Galatians 3:2–4 (NLT):

> Let me ask you this one question: Did you receive the Holy Spirit by obeying the law of Moses? Of course not! You received the Spirit because you believed the message you heard about Christ. How foolish can you be? After starting your new lives in the Spirit, why are you now trying to become perfect by your own human effort? Have you experienced so much for nothing? Surely it was not in vain, was it?

Once we choose to follow Christ and grow up in him, we can easily make the Christian life all about following rules. The book of Galatians is about maturity, not perfectionism. Sometimes believers get it switched around. Maturity is about lifelong learning and the discovery of God; it's learning to walk in step with the Spirit. Maturity is growing in the fruit of the Spirit—love, joy, peace, patience, kindness, goodness, faithfulness, gentleness, and self-control. Against these, the Bible says, there is no conflict with the law (see Gal. 5:22–23). This is what counts: a life changed by Jesus and a faith that expresses itself in love.

One of the greatest descriptions of love comes from what many call "the love chapter"—1 Corinthians 13. There Paul writes that we can exhibit many virtuous characteristics—we can have great faith, give generously, use our gifts, and even die as a martyr—but if we don't love others, we are nothing and we gain nothing. This, he concluded, is love: "Love is patient and kind. Love is not jealous or boastful or proud or rude. It does not demand its own way. It is not irritable, and it keeps no record of being wronged. It does not rejoice about injustice but rejoices whenever the truth wins out. Love never gives up, never loses faith, is always hopeful, and endures through every circumstance" (vv. 4–7 NLT). If we lived out these distinctions in our world, perhaps Christians would be better known for their love.

This is why Jesus lived outside the box of rules and regulations. He came that we might have life, and life to the fullest (see John 10:10). Life in Jesus equals living and loving.

Maturity is a process of growth as we are "transformed into his image with ever-increasing glory" (2 Cor. 3:18 NIV). It's making progress to become more like Jesus, though most people don't fully become like him on this earth. Still, we aim toward that; Paul even says, "I don't mean to say that I have already achieved these things or that I have already reached perfection. But I press on to possess that perfection for which Christ Jesus first possessed me" (Phil. 3:12 NLT).

The words *just live* brought relief and freedom to me that day in my living room. God graciously simplified my life by taking away the need to strive so that I might live freely. Yet I still had lots to learn about what it meant to "just live." I did not know that to fully experience God's presence, I would have to endure his absence. I was soon to experience the most spiritually challenging period of my entire life.

THE DARK NIGHT

When I was a little girl, I could sense God's presence very easily from time to time. It wasn't something I had to conjure up, nor did I have to create time and space in order to feel his presence. I felt it keenly, not only in those spaces where you expect to sense God but also in everyday life. Country roads, pastures, and creeks made up my world, and it was there that I connected with God. Housework and farm chores even brought a sense of God as I went about those tasks. Life on our rural Pennsylvania farm provided a setting that fed my contemplative soul. I'd find myself talking to God throughout the day.

One Saturday when I was in junior high, I was helping clean out the chicken houses, preparing for the next batch of chicks to arrive. (When I say *batch*, I'm talking thousands of chicks. Every eight weeks, my dad raised 156,000 broiler chickens for meat, not egg laying. When the chickens reached their target weight, they were shipped to the poultry plant, eventually ending up in the meat department of local grocery stores. So every eight weeks, we had to clean the chicken houses, haul manure, clean the automatic feeders and waterers by hand, and perform other sanitizing efforts.) I had just gone into the house to fill my bucket with fresh, scalding water, necessary to get the hard-crusted grime off the bell-shaped watering trough. I vaguely recall my three brothers fighting about something. Maybe it wasn't a serious argument, but as I headed back toward the chicken houses, I paused, set my bucket down, and bowed my head, asking God to take care of the situation with my brothers. I'm sure it was a

MATURITY IS A PROCESS OF GROWTH AS WE ARE "**TRANFORMED** INTO HIS IMAGE WITH EVER-INCREASING GLORY."

2 corinthians 3:18 (NIV)

minor incident, because that's all I remember. Brothers fight, and since I had no sisters, I probably carried the emotional weight of our sibling rivalries. Even so, the incident demonstrates that I was aware of God's presence even in the mundane things of life.

Throughout the subsequent years of college, marriage, raising children, and local church ministry, seasons of difficulty came along with life, but God's presence was always near. His Word was dear to me. During our last pastorate, I remember sitting in a booth at a coffee shop across from a woman who wanted to meet with me because she knew my heart for prayer. She was a life coach who helped people find their passion in their career. At one point she said, "I know what you're passionate about! It's obvious that you love the Word. You light up when you talk about the Bible."

But there came a time, just before my forty-ninth birthday, when a dark night began. It lasted a long time, over a decade, although I wouldn't have been able to define it as such at the time. About five years into that period, I was reading some fascinating thoughts written by a sixteenth-century Carmelite friar and priest, John of the Cross. *The Dark Night of the Soul*, written from a prison cell during his own dark night, deals in part, with the seven deadly sins.[1] He suggests that Christians can misuse their spirituality, which was a revelation to me.

The seven sins and the descriptions John gave them caught me by surprise because they are not the sins we would normally think of. It's important for Christians to examine their hearts concerning each one in order to guard against a pharisaical attitude. I know I needed to do so. Our spirituality can go in the wrong direction, and John writes that it often takes a "dark night of the soul" to uproot spiritual sins.

He explains that when a person is a new Christian, God nurtures their soul the way a loving mother cares for and comforts her infant. This is a delightful phase of spiritual growth. I remember such a stage in my life. It is characterized by an eagerness to grow, to learn of God and his ways. There is much

Focus on how great and how deserving God is.

joy in this stage, like that brought by a newborn baby. This new life is exciting, and we want to tell everybody the news of spiritual birth. There's a craving for the Scriptures, to do whatever it takes to know God more and more. But, John warns, there will come a time when God, out of his love, removes the comforts of infancy. He weans us from those things that we hold tightly to in the spiritual walk—even from himself.

John names the seven sins as secret pride, spiritual greed, spiritual luxury, spiritual wrath, spiritual gluttony, spiritual envy, and spiritual sloth. Four of these caught my attention:

Secret Pride. This sin occurs when we become too confident in our spirituality and content with our own growth, thereby creating an unteachable spirit. Like the Pharisees, we compare and then condemn others who are not as spiritual as us. We make light of our sins, not wanting to appear imperfect. This sin leads us to do spiritual exercises to be esteemed by others; we want them to recognize our spirituality.

The contrast to this sin is humility, characterized by looking at ourselves with sober judgment and understanding that religious exercises do not make us holy. Instead, we should "focus on how great and how deserving God is,"[2] which gives us a healthy perspective of ourselves.

Spiritual Greed. This sin occurs when we become dissatisfied with what God does for us. We become greedy for those things that give us good feelings spiritually. If God doesn't give us what we want, we become frustrated with our spirituality. We are more caught up with the emotions that a devotional life gives us, rather than the relationship that spiritual practices nurture. Highly valuing those things considered religious or holy can create an unhealthy attachment that keeps our eyes off the One who is our salvation.

The contrast to this sin is setting our eyes on Jesus, not on outward things or inward experiences. Sometimes these things have to be removed in order for a soul to grow.

Spiritual Wrath. This sin occurs when anger and bitterness set in after the benefits of the spiritual life are taken away. "Some become angry with themselves at this point, thinking this lack of joy is the result of something they have done or neglected to do."[3]

The contrast to this sin is patience in waiting for whatever God gives us, whenever he chooses to give it.

Spiritual Gluttony. This sin occurs when "souls become addicted to the spiritual sweetness of the devotional life and *strive* (my emphasis) to obtain more and more of it. They pass beyond the limits of moderation and nearly kill themselves with spiritual exercises," doing these things not for God but for themselves, and for this reason they grow weary. "It is probably better for these persons to give up their devotions entirely."[4]

The contrast to this sin is to know the invisible, unfathomable, and unfelt grace of God that is much greater than any addiction to spiritual exercises.

John of the Cross wrote, "God perceives the imperfections within us,"[5] yet he loves us in spite of our weaknesses. But he isn't satisfied to leave us there because he knows how much we'll benefit when we come to grips with what we've made of our spirituality. It's for this reason that God gives us a dark night. This explanation might be baffling to those who haven't experienced the dark night, but if you have, you will completely identify with John's words.

During my ten-year-long dark night, I wondered if it was ever going to end. I missed God's presence. I couldn't sense him. My faith stayed intact, though it was challenging and I had lots of questions. It was a faith like I had never had before, one that had no emotional or feeling side to it. I'm not a terribly expressive person, but this faith without feeling, without a sense of his presence, was more like abandonment. I felt as if God had left me.

In the dark night, believing, trusting, praying, and worshiping with a heart numb to his presence was not easy. In fact, my prayer life was minimal, and time in the Word was insignificant. I wanted it to be different, to go back to what I once knew, to experience his presence in prayer and in the Scriptures, but my heart was blank. During that time, more often than not, whenever I participated in spiritual exercises, alone or with others, it was out of an unfelt faith. I had to let God be God. It was like telling someone you love them but feeling no love. Oh, there were a few times, moments really, when his presence came to me, but they were always short-lived.

In August of 2014 I began to feel God's presence again. I was visiting our daughter and her family in Christchurch, New Zealand, when I noticed a book lying on her bedside table titled *The Helper*, by Catherine Marshall.[6] My daughter had recently read it, and she had told me of the impact it had on her life. At the onset of my dark night, I had been influenced by one of Catherine Marshall's other books, *Beyond Ourselves*.[7] It seemed ironic that a decade later, here lay another Marshall book, in my daughter's home in New Zealand. Books feed my intellectual pathway to connecting with God, so, longing to feel him again, I began to read *The Helper*, a book on the Holy Spirit's presence and work in our lives.

The contrast to this sin is to know the invisible, unfathomable, and unfelt grace of God that is much greater than any addiction to spiritual exercises.

Over the weeks of my visit, the book continued to speak into my heart. One morning while sitting alone in a coffee shop, I began to read a chapter titled "Hungering and Thirsting for Something More." I tuned out the peripheral noise of people chatting over coffee and the hissing steam of the latte machine, and I leaned in with hope. It didn't take long for the words to tumble into my heart. God's presence was so evident. There was no doubt it was him. His presence is so tender and warm. He is always a God of loving and gracious conviction, not one of condemnation. *Could I be seeing the light at the end of the tunnel?* my heart questioned.

I resonated with Marshall's prayer at the end of the chapter:

> Lord, I do not want to waste the years left to me on this earth. Nor do I want to go through life as a spiritual beggar, in rags, subsisting on the leftovers and the crumbs when I can be a child of the King. . . . Yet Lord, I know that the gift of the Spirit is not for my joy alone; rather He is given as power for service. You alone can kindle in my heart the deep, fervent desire to be used *like that*. . . . Give me Your own holy passion. Thank You, Lord. Amen.[8]

Tears welled up, and, right there, on August 5, in that coffee shop in Christchurch, God's presence began to emerge in my heart, something I hadn't felt for a long time. Was the dark night over? It had been too long, this dark place in my soul, but the light of his presence began to emerge within.

I didn't care that there, as I sat among coffee shop patrons, tears ran down my face. I began to write feverishly about what I was feeling in my heart:

> *Even now, I can feel my spirit being refreshed, renewed, as His Spirit lovingly, gently, and graciously comes to me. No wonder my word for the*

*year is in. It seemed so little, too small, so insig-
nificant, but I knew it was for me, and even there
the Spirit was making ready my spirit for His work
in my life in 2014.*

God was doing his work in me through the dark night.
I eventually came out of the dark night a changed person.
The biggest difference was the love and grace I had for
others, and the love and grace I had for myself, both of
which I continue to learn and grow in. John of the Cross
described how God takes away our vices in the dark night,
only to create virtues within us. "Through the dark night
pride becomes humility, greed becomes simplicity, wrath
becomes contentment, luxury becomes peace, gluttony
becomes moderation, envy becomes joy, and sloth
becomes strength."[9] By experiencing this dark night in
my soul, I had learned to "just live" in a deeper, more
authentic way.

We can actually become too spiritual, according to
John of the Cross. I would never have thought so, but I
now know it to be true. Could this be true of the North
American church? We need to examine ourselves. Is there
any offensive way in us? Cleanse us, O Father! Take the
words that John of the Cross used to describe cardinal
sins—pride, greed, wrath, luxury, gluttony, envy, and
sloth. Now add the word *spiritual* to each one. Perhaps the
prayer of the psalmist is fitting: "Search me, O God, and
know my heart; test me and know my anxious thoughts.
Point out anything in me that offends you, and lead me
along the path of everlasting life" (Psalm 139:23–24 NLT).
Perhaps we need to heed the words of John of the Cross:

"A soul will never grow until it is able to let go of the tight grasp it has on God."[10] Is the tight grasp we have on God offending those around us who so desperately need to know of God's love, mercy, and grace? Is the tight grasp we have on God offending God himself?

In the middle of my soul-searching, the thoughts from John of the Cross assured me the dark night, though at times incredibly difficult, was God's best for me, that a "faith in the invisible and unfelt grace of God"[11] was far better than checking off my spiritual to-do list. This, as well as Paul's letter to the church of Galatia, was significant in helping me to understand and embrace God's grace, and what it meant to extend grace to others.

Within the next year, God further provided helpful clarification of what it meant to "just live." First, he gave me a new understanding of the word *yoke*, and second, he helped me discover the concept of life rhythm.

PERSONAL REFLECTION

1. How did you respond to the idea that we should "just live"? Do you agree or disagree? Why?

2. Where might you have a pharisaical attitude—harboring a judgmental spirit, pointing an accusatory finger, making rules the top priority?

3. How do you relate to Galatians 3:2–4? In what ways are you trying to be perfect by your own effort rather than living in the freedom, life, and love of the Spirit? Where

might you be living by rules and regulations rather than the fruit of the Spirit?

4. Have you ever experienced a dark night of the soul? What vices did God remove from you during that time? What virtues did God create in you?

6

THE YOKE

discovering the freedom to love

The secret of the easy yoke is simple, actually. It is the intelligent,
informed, unyielding resolve to live as Jesus lived in all aspects
of life, not just in the moment of specific choice or action.

—Dallas Willard, *The Spirit of the Disciplines*

I had been meditating on Matthew 11:28–30, and praying
it into my husband's life. As the lead pastor of a local church,
he was a busy man. Trying to manage time for staff, sermon
preparation, interaction with people, and Sunday worship,
not to mention time with his family, could be wearisome. This
passage, which speaks of taking on Jesus' yoke, one that is
easy and light, seemed a fitting prayer for him.

> Come to me, all of you who are weary and carry
> heavy burdens, and I will give you rest. Take my
> yoke upon you. Let me teach you, because I am
> humble and gentle at heart, and you will find rest

for your souls. For my yoke is easy to bear, and the burden I give you is light. (NLT)

I'll never forget the weekday I was sitting alone in our church auditorium, praying this very Scripture over my husband. One of the staff members came walking through and, in the quietness of the moment, stopped by the pew I was sitting in to say hello. It was his usual check-in to see how things were going. Pete is one of those guys that can probe into your soul. His questions brought my attention to the Matthew 11 passage in a new way.

"You know what Jesus is talking about when he refers to the yoke in that passage?" Pete asked, assuming that I knew. Pete was one of the teaching team pastors at our church, and we called him our resident Hebrew scholar. Short in stature, he stood next to me with his hand on the end of the wooden pew, waiting for my response.

"I only know what I've heard many times," I responded. "The yoke refers to the wooden beam used to pair up oxen in order for them to pull a wagon or a plow. It means I'm on one side of the yoke, and Jesus is on the other. Jesus and me, pulling through life together."

Pete showed me something different. The yoke, he clarified, not only depicted the wooden beam placed on oxen, the most common imagery used in teaching this passage, but it had another meaning as well. The Hebrew word for *yoke* in the Old Testament Scriptures referred to oppression or slavery.

I am the LORD your God, who brought you out of the land of Egypt so you would no longer be their slaves. I broke the yoke of slavery from your neck so you can walk with your heads held high. (Lev. 26:13 NLT)

In that day the LORD will end the bondage of his people. He will break the yoke of slavery and lift it from their shoulders. (Isa. 10:27 NLT)

I led Israel along with my ropes of kindness and love. I lifted the yoke from his neck, and I myself stooped to feed him. (Hos. 11:4 NLT)

Now I will break the yoke of bondage from your neck and tear off the chains of Assyrian oppression. (Nah. 1:13 NLT)

So why are you now challenging God by burdening the Gentile believers with a yoke that neither we nor our ancestors were able to bear? (Acts 15:10 NLT)

As Pete continued to explain these Scriptures to me, he used this word: *expectations*. My ears perked up. My heart skipped a beat. Expectations? He said the word *yoke* also stood for the expectations we place on ourselves or that others place on us—the *should* and *ought* that rise from duty and obligation.

I was seeing this passage like never before. The image of the yoke in my mind went from a wooden beam placed on two oxen to a person weighed down by rules and expectations. This passage was as much for me as my husband.

I pictured myself bent over by dutiful elements of the Christian life, those unattainable rules that I couldn't live up to.

A NEW REALITY

After the conversation with Pete, I looked further into the meaning of Matthew 11:28–30. William Barclay, a Scottish author, theologian, and professor, wrote seventeen volumes of commentary on the New Testament. Ironically, at least for me, his commentaries are called *The Daily Study Bible*. Though I don't read it daily, I enjoy reading his thoughts alongside Scripture. It is said that he wrote for the ordinary reader, and I find his words to be practical for life. When giving his thoughts on Matthew 11, Barclay named six accents he heard from the voice of Jesus. When it comes to verses 28 through 30, the yoke passage, Barclay described Jesus' accent as one of compassion. Barclay wrote: "Jesus spoke to men desperately trying to find God and desperately trying to be good, who were finding the tasks impossible and who were driven to weariness and to despair."[1]

This sounded like me. Trying to do it right. Trying to follow the rules. The chronic defeat often led to despair. Jesus was speaking to the conscientious Jews of his day who were weighted down by so many rules and regulations. What good news this must have been for them.

No wonder Jesus said these words with compassion. He empathized with those who were weary and drained by burdens, the expectations and constraints that placed a heavy load on those who were trying to live rightly. Jesus offered something very different from following rules; he offered peace, rest, and freedom, the very opposite of weariness. He offered himself.

If I had been listening to Jesus that day over two thousand years ago when he spoke these words, I think something would have clicked in my brain. "Wait Jesus, can You repeat what You just said?" I don't think I would have believed what my ears were hearing, especially if I was living under the burden—or yoke—of rules and regulations required by Jewish tradition.

"Did I hear you right? Did you say your yoke is easy and light?"

I can imagine Jesus responding, "Yes, that's exactly what I said. I'm not harsh or condemning, pointing the finger of accusation and judgment. No, I'm here to come alongside you, to teach you, to show you a way that is free and light. It's not oppressive or heavy. You'll find that there is something I require of you, but it will be different than what you think."

When Pete helped me understand the meaning of Jesus' words, I was in a relationship with Jesus that was very real to me, but it was based on trying to live up to what I thought was expected in terms of spiritual growth. Those expectations were sapping the life and joy out of me. Jesus offered his companionship, counsel, and care. I pictured myself as a small child, climbing up on his lap. No expectations, no cravings for spiritual to-dos. Only contentment and rest in the arms of the One who loves me most.

I'm not the rebellious type. I lean more toward compliance, but perhaps compliance has its faults too. In my relationship with Jesus, I allowed the rules and expectations of others, and those I placed on myself, to cast a shadow on my walk with Jesus. Jesus spoke of this very thing when teaching the crowds and his disciples, as told in Matthew 23. The scribes and Pharisees, he pointed out, "crush people with unbearable religious demands and never lift a finger to ease the burden" (v. 4 NLT). The chapter records a fairly long discourse on this subject. Jesus wanted to make sure he got his point across. I can imagine that he spoke with passion about what he knew to be a religious barrier to the relationship he was offering, one that he would give his life for. Jesus was offering so much more than external observances and acts. He warned the scribes and Pharisees with this: "First wash the inside of the cup and the dish, and then the outside will become clean, too" (v. 26 NLT).

> **I was in a relationship with Jesus that was very real to me, but it was based on trying to live up to what I thought was expected in terms of spiritual growth.**

Barclay poses these questions to help evaluate any spiritual practice or ritual of religion.

- Does it make it wings to lift a man up, or a deadweight to drag him down?
- Does it make it a joy or a depression?

- Is a man helped by his religion or is he haunted by it?
- Does it carry him or does he have to carry it?[2]

If spiritual practices or rituals are only done out of duty, to meet the expectation of others, or to earn favor with God, then, according to Barclay, our faith "becomes a depressing affair of burdens and prohibitions."[3]

As I read Barclay's comments for the first time, the answers I gave to these questions clearly showed my attempt to follow a formula that was dragging me down. Though I enjoyed God's presence in my life, the practices expected of me didn't give me wings to fly. Rather, I felt tormented by the heavy weight of expectations.

A NEW COMMANDMENT

Several years ago, while memorizing the book of Ephesians, I was struck by Paul's words explaining the significance of Jesus' life:

For Christ himself has brought peace to us. He united Jews and Gentiles into one people when, in his own body on the cross, he broke down the wall of hostility that separated us. He did this by ending the system of law with its commandments and regulations. He made peace between Jews and Gentiles by creating in himself one new people from the two groups. Together as one body, Christ reconciled both groups to God by means of his death on the cross, and our hostility toward each other was put to death.

He brought this Good News of peace to you Gentiles who were far away from him, and peace to the Jews who were near. Now all of us can come to the Father through the same Holy Spirit because of what Christ has done for us. (2:14–18 NLT)

Jesus came to take away the yoke of the law, the yoke of sin, the yoke of all the rules and regulations. He did away with the old system with its laws, sacrifices, and commandments. He, himself, made a new way—the way of love. Love trumped law. But this was not just any old love. Love incarnate in the person of Jesus, who sacrificed himself for our salvation once and for all. To love became the sole commandment. We are no longer under the law but under grace.

An expert in religious law once asked Jesus what the greatest commandment was. His motive was not pure, as he wanted to discredit Jesus with the question. But Jesus answered his trick question masterfully: "'You must love the LORD your God with all your heart, all your soul, and all your mind.' This is the first and greatest commandment. A second is equally important: 'Love your neighbor as yourself.' *The entire law and all the demands* of the prophets are based on these two commandments" (Matt. 22:34–40 NLT, emphasis mine). Did you catch that? The *entire law* is based on these two commandments. Loving God and loving others is what everything is based on.

What is it to love God with all my heart, soul, and mind? It is to love him with my total being. That requires a love that breathes into my emotions, saturates my thoughts, and impacts my actions. And from this total love for God, we are able to truly love ourselves. The truth that I am a beloved child of God, accepted, forgiven, and loved, seals within my heart a security and significance that enables me to love others freely. Loving self and others is rooted in the love of God.

LOVE VERSUS LOYALTY

It was the last night the disciples would gather together with Jesus before his arrest (see John 13). This motley crew had spent the past three years together. They knew Jesus well. They had watched him heal the sick, the blind, the lame. They had heard his teachings and stories over and over again. They had observed his love for the despised, the forsaken, and the outcast. They had been floored by his loving forgiveness extended to the prostitute, the adulterer, and the criminal. They'd been amazed at his miracles and watched him give people a fresh start, something they had experienced themselves when they chose to follow him.

Yet only after his death and resurrection would they begin to understand the God-man they'd shared life with for three brief years. He knew their hearts, their faults, their unique personalities, their temptations. And yet, as John describes, "[Jesus] had loved his disciples during his ministry on earth, and now he loved them to the very end"

(John 13:1 NLT). He loved even Judas, who was about to betray him, and Peter, who would deny him three times before the light of dawn.

This is always a reassuring thought for me. Jesus loves me in spite of my shortcomings, my failures, and my idiosyncrasies. My sin grieves him, but he loves me too much to let me wallow in it, knowing its destructive power in my life and on other people. Broken by the knowledge of my sin, I receive his love and allow his Spirit to transform me.

In his commentary on John 8, William Barclay writes concerning the adulterous woman brought to Jesus by the religious leaders: "In Jesus there is the gospel of the second chance. He was always intensely interested, not only in what a person had been, but also in what a person could be. He did not say that what they had done did not matter; broken laws and broken hearts always matter; but he was sure that every man has a future as well as a past."[4]

Often, people want to leave the past in the past. "Why bring it up?" they ask. "What's the point in dredging up something I can't do anything about? It's done. It's over." In those conversations, I sometimes use the term *redemptive remembering*,[5] particularly when connecting dots from the past to the present. As much as we hate to admit it, the past does impact the present. But remembering in order to change the present can have a redemptive effect.

My father-in-law loves quotes. When I first met him almost forty years ago, he had a business card with a quote printed on the back that has stayed with me all these years. It held so much meaning for life, especially when I considered how the God of second chances works in our lives. "No one can go back and make a brand-new start; anyone can start now and make a brand-new end."[6] Paul explains this to the believers in Corinth when he writes, "This means that anyone who belongs to Christ has become a new person. The old life is gone; a new life has begun!" (2 Cor. 5:17 NLT).

My husband preached an Easter message once called "The Mulligan God." Mulligan is a golf term that means an extra stroke taken after a poor shot. The first shot isn't counted on the scorecard. God is the God of do-overs. He forgives the "poor shot"—that destructive stroke of sin, maybe a moment, possibly years—and doesn't count it against us.

Little did the disciples know on that night of their final dinner with Jesus that what was about to happen would change the course of history for all human-kind. Knowing his death was near, Jesus washed each of the disciples' feet. There's no way I'd be in a serving mood if I knew my death was near. But Jesus wanted to model, one more time, what it meant

The truth that I am a beloved child of God, accepted, forgiven, and loved, seals within my heart a security and significance that enables me to love others freely.

when he said, "For even the Son of Man came not to be served but to serve others and to give his life as a ransom for many" (Mark 10:45 NLT).

The disciples were blown away by such a humble act, especially Peter, who had no idea how much he would be in need of Jesus' spirit of love and grace that very night. Jesus cupped his hands in the water, washing the grime and dust off the feet of the one who would deny him three times (John 13:7–8).

After dinner, Judas was dismissed to complete his betrayal (which Jesus predicted), then Jesus had final words for the eleven. He began by saying, "So now I am giving you a new commandment: Love each other. Just as I have loved you, you should love each other. Your love for one another will *prove to the world* that you are my disciples" (John 13:34–35 NLT, emphasis mine).

After Jesus had been arrested, Peter was warming himself by the fire in the high priest's courtyard where Jesus was being interrogated. When the rooster crowed in the early morning hours, Jesus heard it among the mocking cries of his accusers. Turning, he looked over at the fire pit where the shrill cry of the rooster had made Peter practically jump out of his skin, remembering the prediction that Jesus had made just hours before. Peter turned to look at Jesus expecting an I-told-you-so look. But Jesus' eyes met Peter's with compassionate love. Peter left the courtyard a broken man, weeping bitterly, more aware than ever of his need to be washed (see John 18:15–27; Luke 22:54–63).

It might have been several weeks after Jesus' death and resurrection that Peter and six of the other disciples fished all night on the Sea of Galilee. It had been Peter's idea to go fishing. Life had changed after Jesus' death and resurrection. It was an uncertain time, and it just made sense to go back to the life they had known as fishermen (see John 21).

At daybreak, someone on the shore called out to them, "Fellows, have you caught any fish?" (John 21:4 NLT). They hadn't. The stranger told them to try fishing on the other side of the boat. When they did, they caught such a net full of fish that they couldn't even pull it onto the boat.

John squinted through the hazy dawn to see who it was on the shore. "It's the Lord!" he shouted. And, as only impulsive Peter would do, he jumped out of the boat and swam to shore, leaving the others to deal with the net full of fish.

Once the disciples arrived on the shoreline, with the full net, they found that Jesus had cooked breakfast. Perhaps they were still sitting around the embers after eating when Jesus directed his thoughts toward Peter.

"Simon son of John," Jesus said, his eyes looking into Peter's, "do you love me more than these?"

Though the other disciples couldn't help but listen in, this conversation was meant only for Peter. We can only surmise what Jesus meant by "more than these." Perhaps he spread his arms to span the shoreline, with the fishing boat and the recent catch. For all we know, Jesus may have been taking Peter back three years when he called him and his brother, Andrew, to follow him in this same place on the shores of Galilee. Perhaps he was once again asking Peter to be a "fisher of men."

Peter looked out over the Sea of Galilee, the boat, and the net full of fish. "Yes, Lord," Peter said, "you know I love you."

"Then feed my lambs."

While Peter mulled over the question, Jesus asked again, "Simon son of John, do you love me?"

Possibly Peter was self-conscious by now, in front of the others. "Yes, Lord," Peter replied, "you know I love you."

"Then take care of my sheep."

Peter, perhaps ready to move on from the conversation, realized Jesus wasn't finished when a third question was asked. "Simon son of John, do you love me?"

By now Peter was hurt. *Why would the Lord ask me three times?* Peter wasn't budging from his answer. "Lord, you know everything. You know that I love you."

"Then," Jesus replied, "feed my sheep."

It might have been later, when Peter was thinking back over this conversation, that it all made sense to him. Three denials. Three restorative questions. Three affirmations of love. Three reminders of his calling.

Peter had been committed to Jesus, even willing to die for him (or so he thought), but three denials told a different story. Peter's fierce profession of loyalty had changed to "I don't even know Him." And, so, on that morning by the shores of Galilee, Jesus asked Peter the same question three times over. Jesus desired love, not just loyalty. He didn't challenge Peter by asking, "Peter, are you committed to me?" or "Are you loyal to me?" No, the question was, "Do you love me?" Loyalty, or allegiance to Jesus, is important, but loyalty alone is not enough. Love binds one heart to another with a grip that will not let go. Love is supreme. Jesus knew love would hold Peter strong in the future—both in his care and feeding of the flock and through his death. These declarations of Peter's love surpassed his self-serving pledges of loyalty. He was now humbly aware of his limitations. For the rest of his life, his love for Jesus would be undeniable.

THE YOKE OF LOVE

Interestingly, Jesus doesn't say, "Come to me, and I will remove all your yokes." Instead he encourages us to take his yoke, one that he describes as "easy to bear." So what is Jesus' yoke? What does he want us to learn from him?

As I think about Jesus' "new commandment" and his questions to Peter, I wonder if Jesus is asking us to take on the yoke of love. He speaks of himself as "humble and gentle at heart" (Matt. 11:29 NLT), not like the Pharisees who placed such heavy, unattainable burdens on their people and judged them when they didn't measure up. Could the yoke of love be the ease and lightness of which he speaks?

But love isn't always easy, you might say. And you'd be right. It's not easy to love those who don't love me. It's hard to love those different from me. It's difficult to love those who hurt me. I'd rather hold grudges. I'd rather stay angry. I'd rather not forgive. Yet Jesus invites us to come to him because only in him are we able to love, and then we are able to love even our enemies. He challenges us to forgive what seems like an unrealistic number of times, and he gives the grace to do so. Jesus knows that bitterness robs us of life and joy, and spills over into the lives of others. He calls us to come and learn from him because he is the greatest example of love. He is the one who empowers us to love others.

And sometimes love is sacrificial. Jesus is not asking us to do something he didn't do. He lived love. He died, in love with us. He rose from the dead, loving us so much that he wanted us to be with him beyond this life. Now we are to love as Jesus loved. Our love for one another will prove to the world that we belong to him. We don't need to prove our views or opinions, values or beliefs. If we have anything to prove, it's that we love.

Could this be where we find rest for our souls? By accepting his invitation to come to him, learn from him, and freely live in him? Is it by taking on his "burden" of love for others that we find peace? A soul that does not love is not at rest.

What if our love for God and others was the measurement for our spiritual growth? How well do we love God? How well do we love others? What if we woke up every morning and trusted God to answer this prayer: "What would love have me do today?" What if love were the one and only thing that Jesus required of us?

I do understand the metaphor of the yoke as a burden of weariness and self-sufficiency and Jesus' yoke as rest for the weary. That isn't necessarily a wrong image of our relationship with Jesus. But I have come to understand Jesus' yoke in a different way, one that makes perfect sense in the context of unrealistic expectations to measure up spiritually. I was trying to follow the rules, which left me in bondage. I felt burdened by obligation and duty. More than anything, I wanted freedom from that spiritual angst. Jesus compassionately invited me—and all who are weary, burned out, exhausted, ready to give up, tired of trying to live up to expectations they can't attain—to take on a different yoke. He invites us to take on this one "burden," which is love.

Jesus doesn't measure us by how much we read the Bible, but we can learn of his life and the way he loved through reading the Scriptures. He doesn't even measure us by how often we pray, though through prayer we can hear his voice, learn from him, and know him better. We can learn about Jesus' love from others, in community. We can learn from Jesus as we encounter people who are different than us. We can learn from Jesus when we share with the poor. We can learn from Jesus with the innocence of a child.

Through his words in Matthew 11, Jesus said to me, "This is not what I had in mind for you, Gwen. Come and let Me teach you that life is about loving Me and loving others. Learn from Me and I'll show you how life can be easy and light. Stop trying to measure up. Stop trying to prove yourself. Stop trying to be someone you're not. Stop comparing. You're living in bondage to expectations. You're living under the weight of perfection. When you learn from me, you'll find rest for that weary soul of yours."

With that realization, I was hit with a new reality. Self-imposed and others-imposed spiritual expectations were a yoke that I had carried way too long. I simply needed to come to Jesus, unload the expectations, the spiritual to-dos, and the defeat that I had carried for years, and find relief and rest in his love for me.

Are you tired? Worn out? Burned out on religion? Come to me. Get away with me and you'll recover your life. I'll show you how to take a real rest. Walk with me and work with me—watch how I do it.

Learn the unforced rhythms of grace. I won't lay anything heavy or ill-fitting on you. Keep company with me and you'll learn to live freely and lightly.

—Matt. 11:28–30

Ah, the unforced rhythms of his grace! This passage describes exactly what I yearned for—to live freely and lightly. I was on my way to discover how he had made me to "live freely," on my way to finding a rhythm, unique to me, that didn't feel forced.

PERSONAL REFLECTION

1. Is the idea of the yoke as a sign of oppression a new thought to you? Read Matthew 11:28–30, pondering the passage with this new insight. Be reminded that Jesus spoke these words with the accent of compassion.

2. Take time to consider the four questions from Barclay in evaluating the outcome of your spiritual practices. What do you discover about yourself and your spiritual practices?

3. Read over the conversation Jesus had with Peter on the shore of Galilee (see John 21). Like he did with Peter, Jesus asks you the question, "Do you love me?". How do you answer? Is it love or loyalty that connects you to Jesus?

4. If the only yoke Jesus asks us to carry is the yoke of love, what does that mean to you personally?

7

FEEL THE BEAT

discovering life rhythms

> Rhythm is not about the instrument;
> it's about the cadence.
>
> —Dennis Jackson

My husband was aware of my spiritual angst. He knew how much it weighed on me, and though I was finding freedom through new perspectives, I was still trying to figure out what time with God looked like for me in practical ways. One day Dennis called me from the church office with his usual check-in. He mentioned that he had just finished reading an article that Dave, our connections pastor, had placed on his desk. Dave, an avid and accomplished writer, told Dennis that, though it was an unfinished article, he wanted to share what he was writing about.

"Honey," Dennis told me, "I think you'll find it really interesting and helpful."

That evening Dennis brought the article home, and though Dave never did finish writing it, that two-page article changed my life. I will forever be grateful to Dave for sharing his thoughts on a concept he called "Life Rhythm Theory."[1] I am doubly grateful for his permission to develop the concept in book form.

Life rhythm has nothing to do with generational changes or the cycle of life and death. Nor is it about the seasons of life we go through from infancy to childhood, adolescence to adulthood, midlife to old age. Life rhythm is about *how* we do life. When you think about it, human beings are prone to different rhythms or patterns of living. Some are morning people, others are night owls. Some people love working like crazy for a time, then enjoying extended time off. Others like to have predictable Monday-through-Friday jobs, clocking in and out with regularity each day. Some like to make decisions moment by moment, and others like to lay out their schedule on a calendar, surveying their lives from a month-at-a-glance perspective.

Dave suggested this may be why some activities and personal practices don't click with some of us and others do. Granted, sometimes life circumstances—like stages of family life or a current job situation—force us into a box that is not of our choosing. Young children certainly create regularity to life that can't be avoided. My son recently told me his three-year-old often comes into his and his wife's bedroom in the early morning, standing inches from a face still deep in sleep, and proclaims, "I need food!" You can't leave a three-year-old to fend for himself without wondering what kind of catastrophe will be found in the kitchen! Raising children demands a daily routine that we might not otherwise choose for ourselves. An even more regimented schedule comes when kids reach school age.

Living for very long outside one's normal rhythm can be exhausting. A job outside one's rhythm may be referred to as the "daily grind." We may adopt or adapt to a different life rhythm for a season, or even for the long haul, but it won't feel natural and may come at a cost to our health. As Dave concluded, "Peak efficiency, energy, and satisfaction in life are more likely to be achieved at the kind of life rhythm one 'naturally' is aligned to."[2]

For the first time in my life, I understood my chronic defeat in the area of daily devotional discipline was not because I didn't want to grow and abide in Christ, and it wasn't because I wasn't doing enough. It was because I was trying to force my spiritual practices into a schedule that didn't fit my natural rhythm.

There are three rhythms by which people typically live.

Daily Rhythm. People who live in a daily rhythm love routine. For the most part, each day starts with a plan that stays on course. They do certain things every Monday, every Tuesday, every Wednesday, and so on. Sometimes each weekday looks exactly alike. Clear daily goals are important to folks with a daily rhythm. They gain a sense of fulfillment at the end of the day when they've been able to stick to the plan and check off the to-do list, accomplishing what they set out to do.

Weekly/Monthly Rhythm. People who live by the week or by the month are not as concerned about what they get done in a day as about the goals they accomplish within a week or a month. They like to prioritize their schedules around what's important in order to stay on task. They

I WAS TRYING TO FORCE MY **SPIRITUAL PRACTICES** INTO A SCHEDULE THAT DIDN'T FIT MY NATURAL **RHYTHM**.

love tracking life on a calendar. They might have to ask, "What day is it?" because no one day in their week will look like another, or like that same day the next week.

Seasonal/Yearly Rhythm. People who live life seasonally or by the current year are less concerned about what they accomplish in a day, week, or month and are more concerned about the bigger picture of life. A sense of accomplishment comes from living life with a thematic backdrop that will influence their creativity and production. They hardly ever ask, "What day is it?" because it just doesn't matter to them.

After reading Dave's article a few times, I easily identified my natural rhythm. That was a defining moment as I began to see myself in a new light. This discovery not only gave me permission to settle into and accept a rhythm that was true to myself but also made a difference in my spiritual life. Finally I had found a practical answer for the spiritual angst I had struggled with for so many years.

By teaching "Life Rhythm Theory" in various venues in the mission organization that my husband and I serve, I've seen how freeing this concept is for those burdened by expectations that don't match their natural tendencies. The response has been overwhelming.

Ask any musical person what the two factors in rhythm are and they will say beat and timing. Rhythm is a strong, regular, repeated pattern of movement or sound, and, without it, music isn't music. It's what moves us on the dance floor. It's what gets our hands clapping, our toes tapping, and our heads nodding. I've got rhythm; you have rhythm; we all have rhythm. I'm not talking about musical rhythm, but a rhythm by which we live life. We all have a natural beat to our lives that connects with a sense of time, a rhythm that affects our life in almost everything we do and how we do it. In what rhythm do you live life? Whatever your life rhythm, it will affect how you engage in spiritual formation.

Could it be the concept of life rhythms best explains what many call "pace" when describing the way they manage life? We talk of our fast-paced life or say that we need to change the pace of life. Perhaps we just need to come to terms with the rhythm by which we engage life, then let that rhythm flow according to our natural beat. Life rhythm is the strong, regular, repeated pattern of life. So how do these rhythms play out? In the next chapters, let's explore each life rhythm in depth.

PERSONAL REFLECTION

1. What emotions surface when you read about life rhythms? Why?

2. Given these brief descriptions of the three life rhythms, do you find yourself identifying with one of them? Write down why you see yourself leaning into that particular rhythm. (The next three chapters will show you if your hunch is right.)

3. How do you think the concept of life rhythms might give you a new perspective in your career or in how you view others?

FINDING
YOUR
RHYTHM

part 3

8

SUNRISE, SUNSET

exploring daily rhythm

All in a day's work.
—Anonymous

I grew up on my mom's schedule, a daily schedule. Monday was washday. Tuesday was the day Nana (my mom's mother) came over for dinner. When my three brothers and I were young, Wednesdays and Saturdays were bath nights, unless it was summer. Think 1950s: the farmhouse we moved into when I was four years old didn't have an indoor bathroom. Thursday evenings were designated for grocery shopping. My brothers and I would pile in the car with Dad and Mom and drive to a neighboring town to buy our weekly groceries. When I was in junior high school, I always looked forward to Thursday evenings. While my parents shopped for groceries, my brothers and

I would go to the nearby Grants variety store to browse, often going home with a new 45 rpm record. Saturday was cleaning and baking day. Sunday was always a day for going to church, having hamburgers and french fries for lunch (and not from a fast-food restaurant), and only doing work that was necessary on the farm. It was a day of rest and play.

My mom has had daily devotions for as long as I can remember. Even now that she is eighty-six years old, her rhythm has not changed. Her breakfast place setting not only includes a bowl, spoon, and cereal box, but her Bible, devotional book, and journal. Writing a one-page journal entry has been a routine of hers that has lasted for decades. Every. Single. Day. Now, along with her usual breakfast routine, she reads from her journal about what happened in her life ten and twenty years ago. Now that's what I call routine.

A different daily devotional book lies on Mom's bedside table, and every night at bedtime she reads the devotional for the day. Again, that's something I remember from my childhood. I'd often crawl in bed next to her while she read, waiting for Dad to come in from his nightly farm checks.

Mom worked as an elementary school secretary for twenty-five years. I figure anybody who can last that long at one job must be a daily person. Without much thought, she wakes up in the morning and goes about her usual routine for that day of the week. A daily rhythm fits her best, and though she may have become more relaxed in her schedule with age and decreased responsibilities, it is still evident that she is a daily person. She's been keeping some of these routines for eighty-six years!

Like my mom, daily people function best when they have a system in place. They know what needs to be done and how to get it done, and they usually do get it done. They can accomplish a lot in one day because they have a clear plan and know how to achieve the desired result. "One day at a time," may be the daily person's motto. Each day has its own agenda, and to veer from the plan will cause frustration. They prefer to stay on course or at least be given advance notice of changes. It's not unusual for a daily person to make a to-do list with the realistic goal of getting each item checked off before the end of the day. Spontaneity is rarely a part of their beat.

My husband teases that my mom did spring cleaning *every* Saturday. And, there may be some truth to that. In that one day, between Mom and I, we would get the entire two-story farm house clean, which included dusting, vacuuming, turning kitchen chairs upside down on the table and cleaning off the leg bottoms, mopping the kitchen and bathroom floors, and wiping down the bathroom and kitchen counter tops, appliances, sinks, and tubs. In addition to the cleaning, making Toll House chocolate chip cookies and a Black Joe chocolate cake (named for the cup of coffee in the recipe) was a Saturday staple. Mom still makes that cake, and, in the summer months, we may even get in some yard or garden work.

My mom's daily rhythm played a part in my life long after I left home for college. For the first ten years of my marriage, my mom wrote me a weekly letter describing each day of the past week on the farm. She would actually write the day of the week to start each paragraph, then describe in detail what happened that day, including what they had for dinner. It was her way of sharing life with me from a distance. During those years, Dennis and I lived in Indiana, Michigan, and Texas. We visited central Pennsylvania once a year, and my parents visited us annually until their age made traveling difficult. In my first decade of marriage, I could count on that letter every week, something I appreciate even more now that my own children live a long distance away.

Daily people function best when they have a system in place.

Though I don't have a system for housecleaning like she did, I am grateful for the good work ethic she instilled in me on those cleaning and baking days. Mom's daily time in the Word and in prayer gave her the strength she needed to carry her through some difficult times. Recently she told me she woke up one morning feeling heavy with life's circumstances, but a particular word in her devotional book turned her attitude around, giving her a brighter perspective for the day.

Daily people amaze me. Their discipline is unmatched. They are consistent, steady, and dependable. Once they get their system down, their daily routine provides a stable environment in which they can function confidently and proficiently. In her prime, my mom was a school secretary, a farm wife, and mother of four, and she anchored herself in the daily routine of life. Though life looks different for her now, she still leans into the daily rhythm to order her days.

A QUICK GUIDE TO DAILY RHYTHM

characteristics of daily people
- Their preferred calendar is a page-a-day planner.
- They ask, "What day is it?"
- They are task oriented.
- They accomplish a lot each day.
- They work best with clear, attainable daily goals and responsibilities.
- They find it rewarding to check items off a daily to-do list.
- They love routine tasks.
- They like systems they can use to maximize their efficiency.
- They are interested in the *now*.
- They dislike spontaneity.

offbeat or rhythm issues for daily people
- Long-range forecasting or strategic planning may paralyze them.
- Big-picture thinking is not their forte.

spiritual parallels for daily people
- They gain strength spiritually through daily times with God.
- They prefer routine in how they spend time with God.
- They grow best on a steady diet of time spent in the Word and in prayer.
- They may be frustrated when they don't discover new spiritual insights or experience faster growth.

- They reflect best on their growth by looking in the rearview mirror.
- They may not enjoy a weekend retreat or a day alone with God as much as those who live by a different rhythm.

cautions for daily people

- They may become legalistic in their daily practices and expectations.
- They may appear to be (or they may actually become) self-righteous because of their daily discipline.
- They must remember that consistency in discipline does not necessarily equal intimacy with Christ.
- They may need to change up their routine occasionally to maintain freshness.

PERSONAL REFLECTION

1. Are you a daily person? If so, what does that look like for you?

2. If you don't consider yourself a daily person, did the description of a daily person remind you of someone you know? How does this new insight change your perspective on this person?

9

WHEN A PLAN COMES TOGETHER

exploring weekly/monthly rhythm

People with goals succeed because they
know where they're going.

—Earl Nightingale

My husband, Dennis is a weekly/monthly person; he lives by his calendar. Every couple of months he will say to me, "Honey, we need to sit down and look at the calendar." He always has a full schedule with frequent travel, in which I join him from time to time. He geeks out about calendars and organizes his schedule in great detail. Just the other day, we sat down to review the calendar. I was on the sofa, computer on my lap, ready to record dates, places, and flight schedules. He sat across from me in a comfy chair with his computer. Sometimes we do this sitting across from each other at a coffee shop, computers back to back as we face one another, our screens open to our calendars.

As we begin to share and compare dates—adding items that have been definitely scheduled and discussing others—I become overwhelmed when we get about three to four months out. We usually review six months at a time, so by the time we finish our calendar "date," I'm heaving big sighs as I try to grasp what we'll be doing for the next six months, one week at a time. Dennis often feels pressured by my sighing, and we sometimes end up in a tiff over a trivial thing, at least to me—a calendar. I'm not a calendar girl. I'm a seasonal girl. I don't live by the rhythm of a weekly or monthly schedule.

Because of Dennis' frequent travel days, his weeks do not look anything alike. But even when he was in pastoral ministry his days and weeks could be different. Sunday is the constant in local church ministry. Every seven days there's a sermon to be preached. While a daily person may set aside certain days of the week for sermon prep, the weekly person may find prep time on whatever day works for them in that particular week. Weekly/monthly people are not as concerned with what they get done on a daily basis as they are with accomplishing a given goal. You might remember the 1980s TV show *The A-team*; it was one of my husband's favorites. The fictional series featured four Vietnam vets who undertook missions to help out innocent people, all while being chased by the authorities for a crime they didn't commit. Upon completion of a mission, the group's leader, Hannibal Smith, would proudly and confidently light a cigar and say, "I love it when a plan comes together." No wonder Dennis liked this show. He takes great satisfaction when a plan comes together, a goal is met, or a project is completed.

When we were in local church ministry, a plan came together every Sunday for Dennis as he delivered a sermon he had prepared or as a theme for the weekend or month came together through worship and media. I'm continually amazed at his capacity to spin multiple plates and, without missing a beat, pick up another project that suddenly needs attention.

Though weekly/monthly people tend to be great jugglers, they may occasionally take on more than they can handle, a confession my husband has made more than once. He often estimates he can get more done than time allows, overcrowding his schedule in an attempt to fit it all in. When reality sets in, it can cause frustration. It is important for weekly/monthly people to set realistic goals, and bouncing proposed deadlines off others can help set reasonable boundaries.

A weekly/monthly person will get bogged down by the seemingly tedious routines that daily people thrive on. For the weekly/monthly person, one day in a week may not look like any other day in that week, or even like that same day in the following week. Filling a daily quota doesn't matter to them nearly as much as seeing the overall progress of a project as it moves toward completion. It's not unusual for weekly/monthly people to schedule a pause in their week or month, giving their minds a rest from current projects. In the pastorate, Sundays were not a day off for Dennis, so he chose Friday as his down day. When the kids were in school, we looked forward to having lunch together and doing whatever made sense for that particular day.

This rhythm plays out in a weekly/monthly person's spiritual growth as well. For instance, Dennis has been taking a day alone with God about once a month for years now. These entire days are devoted to seeking God and have been beneficial to his spiritual growth. Dennis marks this time on his calendar (of course!) and finds a quiet place where he can spend the day. Over the years, he has used public libraries, seminary campuses, parks, retreat houses, and prayer rooms for this purpose. He listens to an audio recording of the Scriptures while driving to work on some mornings, but his scheduled days away are what refresh him the most—an entire day of spiritual reflection and growth, once a month.

I recently taught the concept of life rhythms to a church staff and leadership team. The following day, one of the team members sent me an online ad featuring the perfect calendar for the weekly/monthly rhythm. It was a huge, three-by-four-foot wall calendar, with the month spelled out in foot-high black letters. So for each month, the words *It's May* or *It's September* took up most of the enormous page. A tiny calendar appeared in the upper right-hand corner, which the ad explained was "Just in case you need to know what day it is." I smiled at the marketing question, "Why know the date when you could just know the month?" That's exactly the sort of calendar a weekly/monthly person needs.

The production capacity of a weekly/monthly person is unparalleled. Others often remark about their ability to take on big projects and bring them to completion with excellence. Often, such folk are adept at pulling a team together in order to complete the undertaking, but the task itself is what drives them. Nothing makes weekly/monthly people come alive more than accomplishing a task or goal.

EVEN ON
VACATION,
GOALS MATTER
TO THE WEEKLY/
MONTHLY
PERSON.

It's no wonder Dennis loves his calendar. When I came to understand his life rhythm, I began to see why our calendar dates are so important to him. He lives by his calendar because his weeks and months are anchored in the goals that he has set out to accomplish. He and I live life by different beats, as I find many couples do, but having a spouse who is decisive in setting priorities to accomplish the task at hand has been a good complement for my more laid-back nature, and vice versa.

As I write this chapter, we are vacationing near Smoky Mountains National Park. We've enjoyed our hiking days and our days dedicated for reading, watching a movie, and enjoying a table game. The second floor of our cabin has a large room with a pool table. Since everything we've needed is on the main floor, I didn't go upstairs for the first couple days. The first time I made my way upstairs, I found two large Post-it sheets hanging on the wall. I smiled. Walking closer to take a look, I saw Dennis had listed the days of the week on the first sheet and added (in various colors with permanent markers) what we did each day. To the right was another sheet with a list of goals: Hike. Read a book. Hot tub. Dinner out. Tally marks were placed by each objective reached. Even on vacation, goals matter to the weekly/monthly person.

I've been married to this man since 1978. The intentionality he has brought to our lives from the start has generated more purpose and given more meaning to life than I could have ever imagined.

A QUICK GUIDE TO
WEEKLY/MONTHLY RHYTHM

characteristics of weekly/monthly people

- Their preferred calendar is a week or month at a glance.
- They ask, "What month is it?"
- They are goal oriented.
- They are driven to achieve big goals or complete major projects.
- They enjoy long-term projects.
- They love to organize their schedule and set priorities.
- They are more concerned about accomplishing goals than about checking off items on daily to-do lists.
- They enjoy spontaneity.
- They have a great capacity to take on new projects, even when very busy.
- For them, no day in their week looks like another day in that same week.
- They value weekends and monthly breaks.

offbeat or rhythm issues for weekly/monthly people

- Daily, routine tasks hamper their style.
- They sometimes struggle to accomplish the daily processes required to complete a project.
- They may enjoy committing to a project more than completing it.
- They are inclined to take on more than they can handle.

spiritual parallels for weekly/monthly people

- They enjoy Sundays as a pause from what may be a forced daily routine.
- They gain strength when spending extended periods focused on spiritual growth, such as specific days away or a retreat.
- They may think a few minutes spent on a spiritual discipline isn't long enough.

cautions for weekly/monthly people

- They may find it too easy to put off tasks and then play catch-up.
- They may make plans they never act on.
- They may overschedule.

PERSONAL REFLECTION

1. Are you a weekly/monthly person? If so, what does that look like for you?

2. If you don't consider yourself a weekly/monthly person, did the description of a weekly/monthly person remind you of someone you know? How does this new insight change your perspective on this person?

10

THE YEAR OF JUBILEE

exploring seasonal/yearly rhythm

> For everything there is a season,
> a time for every activity under heaven.
> —Ecclesiastes 3:1 NLT

By now you know I'm not a daily person, and I do not live my life by a weekly/monthly rhythm either. Though I adapted to my mom's daily routine growing up, it wasn't my natural rhythm. I live best by a seasonal/yearly rhythm.

A start and finish is important to a seasonal person. Committing to something indefinitely will wear them down. Knowing there is an end in sight will give them assurance that "this won't last forever." They tend to take in two or three months at a time, processing what is happening in life, then understanding where God is working or moving. They like to look at the bigger picture of life, allowing the ebb and flow of the seasons to set the course for a particular end. They are not driven by to-do lists, priorities, or calendars, but rather ask what activities, events, resources, or people can make a particular season effective and meaningful toward personal or spiritual growth.

Looking back over my life, I can see that pattern playing out in a variety of ways, as far back as childhood. I remember loving summers, when I could walk in pastures and play along creeks, free of strict schedules, school days, and nightly homework. When fall rolled around, it didn't take long for the Monday through Friday school schedule to get the best of me. Honestly, I love to learn, but the daily routine sapped my energy until the next holiday break came along. Even then, the break was never long enough to satisfy. Before I knew it, I was back to getting up early and running down our country road to catch the school bus at 6:30.

The closest thing I've ever had to a clock-in/clock-out job was the three years after I graduated from high school. I worked in two different medical facilities as a licensed practical nurse. Neither of them lasted beyond a season or a year. The first job, working the night shift at a nursing home, lasted nine months. A friend, who was working a nine-to-five job at the time, was as done with her routine as I was with mine. We signed up for a summer adventure that took us to Brazil. There we built a floating hangar on a branch of the Amazon River for a Wycliffe missionary's pontoon plane. It was a summer to remember, and one that changed my life. I had never seen myself as college material, but in the Brazilian jungle I sensed God had more for my life. I knew then the next step was to pursue a college degree.

When I went off to college, I thrived on its flexible schedule. Mapping my life in semesters fit right into my seasonal rhythm. I could wrap my head around blocks of time that had a beginning and an end. Summer was a respite from studies and gave opportunity for a brand-new season.

Once married, children started coming along beginning the first year. Being a mom kept me more than busy, especially when I was still in college. Later, while I was finding my ministry niche in the churches my husband and I served, raising four children occupied most of my time. Once the kids began school, September always brought on the morning, afternoon, and evening routines that kept everybody on track. When summer rolled around, I was as ready to be done with the school year as the kids were. Three months of flexibility—unhurried mornings, afternoons at the beach on nearby Lake Michigan, the ease of taking life leisurely—were a welcome relief from the school routine.

While raising our family, I incorporated once-a-month grocery shopping into my planning. Weekly shopping bogged me down, and though I'm not a monthly person, I found that spontaneous shopping doesn't work well when you have a growing family. Now, I pick groceries up as needed, which is easier as an empty nester.

The seasonal/yearly person gets burned out on repetition and weighed down with routine. I'm a runner, but that activity has its seasons too. Sometimes I'll take a couple of months off and then pick it up again, especially before a race I've registered for. I don't wash my hair every day. I don't always shower every day. I might eat breakfast or I might not. I'm tidy and organized, but there definitely is no cleaning routine in our home. The bathrooms get cleaned when they need it. I don't follow the every-Saturday cleaning and baking schedule that I grew up with. I bake when I feel like baking or if we are having company. My kitchen floor gets mopped about twice a year. (Mom, just so you know, I do spot clean if necessary, but the entire kitchen floor? Yep, about twice a year. Love you, Mom!)

Understanding my life rhythm has given me the freedom to connect with God in a seasonal way. I confessed at the start of this book that I don't read my Bible every day. Seasonal people tend to go with the flow of life. What is going on in a particular season will determine how a seasonal/yearly person connects with God during that time. They may choose to read through a book that relates to what God is teaching them, or they may choose to focus on a particular passage of Scripture for a period of time, letting the words soak in deeply. Whatever they choose to do in their God-connection will have relevancy when it fits into the bigger picture of what God is doing in their life.

That season became a time when God sifted and shifted me like never before.

It's no wonder that my earlier journal entries expressed defeat. The occasional entries—both unscheduled and random—were right in line with my seasonal rhythm. It's unfortunate that I lived with defeat for so long. I love to put my thoughts to paper, but it is a rare occasion when I make journal entries on consecutive days.

Because I think seasonally or yearly, I often assign a theme to my spiritual growth. Years ago, I memorized the book of Ephesians over a year and a half, along with a friend who was interested in memorizing Scripture. We each chose a different translation, memorized three verses each week, and met every two weeks to recite what we had already memorized along with six new verses. I read a commentary on the text I was memorizing. It was an exhilarating time in my spiritual life as I came to understand who I was in Christ through the first three chapters, then gleaned insight on how to live out my faith from the apostle Paul's final three chapters of practical encouragement. Slowly digesting one of my favorite books in the Bible over the span of a year and a half was a delight. The words penetrated my heart far deeper than they would have if I had just read a chapter a day for six days.

Not surprisingly for a seasonal/yearly person, an especially dry time followed my season of growth. I felt like the wind had been taken out of my spiritual sails. Dry times can be especially frustrating to the seasonal/yearly person. After a high season of feeling God's presence keenly, finding it difficult to sense his Spirit may cause a seasonal/yearly person to wonder what they did wrong. Awareness, acknowledgement, and acceptance of the dry times are key to getting through them. Dry times will come, and knowing how to navigate the dry season will help the seasonal/yearly person cope until they enter a fresh season. Instead of feeling guilty in the dry times, the seasonal/yearly person can be assured a new season will come in time.

During that dry season, I processed my experience by reading books that were pertinent to my struggles.

Though it wasn't as invigorating as the year and a half when I memorized Ephesians, that season became a time when God sifted and shifted me like never before. Looking back, I can see how the words Paul wrote to the church of Ephesus carried me through that season.

During that time a new friend from Scotland told me about a book called *Praying in Color*.[1] After reading the book, I found a craft store and bought myself a good pencil, a black acid-free marker, watercolor pencils, and a notebook filled with sketch paper. I'd sit on a bench in one of the busiest squares in the city with my notebook and a small pouch filled with art supplies. Sometimes I'd muse on a meaningful Scripture passage and draw an image related to my life, praying as I drew, taking in the Word, filling it in with colors that represented my heart. At other times, I drew pictures that represented a special loved one and my prayer for them. It was a wonderful way for me to relate to God. It was typical of the way seasonal/yearly people find themselves connecting with God in creative or artistic ways.

A seasonal/yearly person finds their anchor in just living life, processing what's going on in the particular season they find themselves in. Once I identify what season I'm in, that helps me wrap my head around the focus of my life for a given time. While reading through the book of James over a matter of six months or so, I felt convicted about combining my faith with action. Was I acting upon my faith? Was I following through on the things I knew God was placing on my heart? Was I listening to God's voice and following his lead? The theme of my season always incorporates itself into my daily life. So, although I don't have daily devotions, the spiritual practices I engage in play out daily.

In addition to reading Scripture that sets the tone for the season, the practice of choosing a word for the year fits well with the spirituality of a seasonal/yearly person. Though it's a practice people of all rhythms can incorporate into their spiritual growth, the seasonal/yearly person especially will find this inspiring as they look at the bigger picture of their life.

Solomon, the writer of Ecclesiastes, may have been a seasonal/yearly person. He seems to bemoan the fact that nothing changes: "The sun rises and the sun sets, then hurries around to rise again" (Eccl. 1:5 NLT). That sounds like someone who gets weary with the regularity of life. Seasonal/yearly people like variety. Yes, the sun rises and sets, but we also live on a planet that makes a yearly orbit around the sun, creating the changing seasons. Every couple of months or so, the seasonal/yearly person needs something new and fresh to keep them in orbit. They find routine tedious.

Discovering my life rhythm has been liberating. My rhythm describes how I enter into life with the most vigor and effectiveness.

It's not uncommon for a seasonal person to struggle with a false guilt about not being daily. Let me say that again. They struggle with a *false* guilt. I've heard this especially from those who have grappled with the expectation they should have daily devotions. If this is the case with you, you may find that a simple daily prayer is helpful. At times, I have found this brief prayer to be grounding: "Father, fill me with Your Spirit for this day." A friend of mine uses this prayer daily: "Holy Spirit, lead me, guide me, go before me this day." Eventually, such a prayer will likely come to feel legalistic, so changing it up for whatever season you're in will keep it fresh for the seasonal person.

When Dennis and I sat together on the calendar date I mentioned in chapter 9, we experienced the tension that occurs when different rhythms collide. Our date ended with the tiff that sometimes happens when I become overwhelmed by Dennis' meticulous schedule and start sighing. I love to travel with Dennis, but this calendar thing just wasn't working, so we looked for a solution for the pressure I felt every time we went over our schedules. Dennis suggested a year-at-a-glance calendar that I could hang on the wall somewhere to gain an overall picture for the year ahead. I immediately felt some relief. It's a little thing, but moving from a monthly to a yearly perspective was a great help. I just needed to see the overall picture, a year at a glance.

Seasonal/yearly people, when they set their mind to it, can tackle a project or task for the long haul. For instance, when I set out to write this book, my mantra was "This is the year of the book." I had some lighter writing seasons throughout the year, but overall it has been a season devoted to writing. Now that it is almost over, I'm diligently writing to finish the work and meet my goal. For the seasonal/yearly person, assigning a project to a season gives purposeful focus and creative productivity.

My birthday falls two weeks before the year's end. Though there may be downsides to having a birthday around the holiday season, I find it fits right into my yearly rhythm. I turn another year older just before the world rings in a new year. Recently I entered a new decade of life. My husband threw a surprise birthday gathering for me, during which he focused on celebrating not the big six-0 but the fact that I had been a Christian for fifty years. He referred to the coming year as the Year of Jubilee, relating to the Leviticus passage in which God instructed the Israelites to count off seven sets of seven years, and then to declare the fiftieth year as the Year of Jubilee. That year was to be set apart as holy, a year to proclaim freedom throughout the land. This thought inspired me for the year ahead. "This is the Year of Jubilee" was my mantra for my sixtieth year; it set the tone for my life, for the bigger picture. Plus, it kept me feeling younger. My husband knew me well!

Discovering my life rhythm has been liberating. My rhythm describes how I enter into life with the most vigor and effectiveness. Just as the seasons come and go— bringing spring flowers, warm summer days, colorful fall leaves, and freshly fallen snow—I, too, need changing seasons to keep me fresh, purposeful, and motivated.

A QUICK GUIDE TO SEASONAL/YEARLY RHYTHM

characteristics of seasonal/yearly people

- Their preferred calendars are year-at-a-glance.
- They ask, "What season (or year) is it?"
- They are process oriented.
- They prefer a big-picture perspective.
- They are good at long-range planning.
- They are more interested in living life than in checking off achievements.
- They often question why others waste time doing things that seem unnecessary to them.
- They can launch into a huge task if it fits into their view of the year ahead.
- They may work feverishly during a highly productive season, which is followed by a less productive season.
- They prefer activities that have defined starting and stopping points.
- They enjoy extended vacations or sabbaticals.
- They are often creative and artistic.

offbeat or rhythm issues for seasonal/yearly people

- They will have trouble engaging in a task or project if a connection can't be made with the bigger picture of life.
- They may find it difficult to manage daily tasks.
- They are often paralyzed by trivial things.
- They find repetition demotivating.

spiritual parallels for seasonal/yearly people
- They are likely to have high and low seasons spiritually.
- They gain strength by engaging in the process of life and seeing how it relates to God.
- They often align well with longer seasons of discipline (such as forty-day fasts or all-night prayer meetings).
- They may enjoy expressing their devotion to God through creative outlets such as art, writing, or music.
- In dry times, they need self-awareness and understanding of what sustains them.
- They may incorporate a very brief God-connection into their daily schedule, but without guilt, knowing they connect with God in many other ways.
- They may be guided by God to be a daily person for a season.

cautions for seasonal/yearly people
- They may be looked upon as lazy, without purpose, and undisciplined when in dry times.
- They may look to the next season for motivation.
- Their excitement about high seasons may produce guilt in others.

PERSONAL REFLECTION

1. Are you a seasonal/yearly person? If so, what does that look like for you?

2. If you don't consider yourself to be seasonal/yearly, did the description of a seasonal/yearly person remind you of someone you know? How does this new insight change your perspective on this person?

11

FREEDOM!

life rhythms in action

So Christ has truly set us free. Now make sure that you stay free,
and don't get tied up again in slavery to the law.

—Galatians 5:1 NLT

That day in the Budapest coffee shop, what began as an email response to Erica turned into an attached document that was five pages long. I related with Erica's struggle to find a God-connection that harmonized with the rhythm of her life, one that didn't feel legalistic or like she was just going through the motions. In my long letter, I shared, on a much smaller scale, some of the biblical insights and personal stories found in this book, along with resources that have been beneficial in understanding how I best connect with God.

Four days later Erica's name popped up in my inbox.

Dear Gwen,

Thank you so much for this letter. You don't know how much this has meant to me. Honestly, I literally wept when I read it, just feeling like there really can be freedom in knowing that I can find my life rhythm and not be continuously living with guilt over not being a daily person.

Three years after the Budapest correspondence, I asked Erica how she sees her seasonal/yearly life rhythm playing out in her spiritual formation. "I really have found freedom from guilt," she said, "knowing what I now know about seasonal life rhythm." Erica has found that participating in various Bible studies—something that has a start and finish to it—provides a seasonal framework that changes things up, adding variety to keep her fresh and motivated.

Erica also discovered some practical tools that have sustained her in the low times, which are not uncommon for the seasonal person. She uses a voice-recording app to record truths about her identity in Christ, then listens to them every day. Doing something every day can have meaning for the seasonal person, if they see how it fits into the overall picture of what God is doing in their life. Erica also finds it helpful to post memory verses on her bathroom mirror as a reminder of God's consistent presence amid the ebb and flow of life.

In my initial letter to Erica, I shared a resource that is helpful in determining how one best relates with God. Gary Thomas's book, *Sacred Pathways*, is a worthwhile read for understanding "your soul's path to God." Seeing yourself in one of the nine pathways suggested can be a helpful accompaniment to finding your life rhythm. One or two pathways may surface as your natural way of connecting with God.[1]

After Erica discovered she connected to the *sensate* pathway, loving God with the senses, she realized how much the Sunday worship services at her church filled her soul. Though she is seasonal, she finds the weekly celebration, especially worshiping through music, gives her strength for the season she finds herself in. "Through God's grace," Erica shared, "I have experienced freedom in this area of my life."

Liberated and *guilt-free* are the descriptive terms I hear most often from those who have discovered their life rhythm. When we try to do spiritual practices in a life rhythm that's not our own, the practices become dogmatic, legalistic, and enslaving. Once a person recognizes they've been trying to fit into a rhythm that isn't natural for them, they gain wings to fly. It's uplifting, life giving, and freeing to understand the ways you best connect with God. No wonder Erica wept through my letter. She was experiencing freedom.

Since that correspondence with Erica, I have had the privilege of teaching "Life Rhythm Theory" workshops to a number of Christian leaders. I continue to hear stories of the freedom people find upon discovering their life rhythm. Most people I hear from are either weekly/monthly or seasonal/yearly people who had been forcing themselves to adopt the spirituality of a daily rhythm. They are now finding grace to live within a rhythm that comes naturally to them. Daily people, upon discovering other life rhythms, find freedom to accept and celebrate the spiritual practices of others who live by a different life rhythm.

Here are some stories of those who have experienced freedom from false guilt and a greater connection with God by understanding and embracing their life rhythm.

JOY

My friend, Joy, and I share the same age but not the same rhythm. When she first heard about life rhythm, she knew immediately she fell into the daily rhythm. It's what she's been doing for years. "I absolutely love the quietness and solitude of an early morning," she told me. "It feels like a gift God made especially for me. Because I'm a morning person, I have the energy needed to concentrate on Bible study and prayer. I'm usually too brain dead by evening to do much more than be grateful."

Joy takes advantage of the time when she is at her best. Not everyone is at their best in the morning. Circadian rhythm, or our body clock, is unique for each of us. Our body clock repeats every twenty-four hours and is quite persistent. That's why we experience jet lag when we travel across time zones. Our body clock is trying to get in sync with the local time. The only time I have any sense of what it feels like to be a morning person is when I'm experiencing jet lag. I rise in the early morning hours, wide awake and ready to go. But once my body clock adjusts, the same built-in rhythm picks up the beat on a twenty-four-hour cycle. Within days, I'm back to my night-owl self.

The discovery of life rhythm has given Joy a greater awareness of the particular characteristics of her five grown children. "Actually, it has helped me to understand and affirm my own children. It's given me a fresh perspective. I love the uniqueness of God's creation and that includes his children."

It's especially important for parents to realize children will not all fall into the same life rhythm category. Just as all children have their own personality, passions, strengths, and talents, they will also have a unique life rhythm. Encouraging them to understand what rhythm drives them and empowering them to connect with God within that rhythm will make it as life giving for them as it is for us.

Joy married the opposite of her life rhythm. "Dan is seasonal. I remember early in our married life being concerned that he didn't seem to have a consistent devotional time. Much later I realized he was continually chewing on a subject or passage for that season."

This concern for the other's spiritual health is common in marriages where the spouses differ in life rhythm. A husband shared with me he dealt with guilt every morning when he watched his wife go into a side room and close the door so she could spend time with God. Discovering his seasonal life rhythm not only freed him from guilt but also gave his wife a grace-filled perspective toward her husband.

Joy doesn't consider herself very organized, but she loves to have "a specific ongoing study for a period of weeks or months," she says. "I've used Bible study aids and devotionals, and other times just dove into the Word.

IT'S ESPECIALLY
IMPORTANT
FOR PARENTS
TO REALIZE
CHILDREN WILL
NOT ALL FALL
INTO THE SAME
LIFE RHYTHM
CATEGORY.

I have always journaled, but I'm not a prolific writer, so this usually consists of short phrases, often bullet points, and short prayers." As a daily person, Joy doesn't like to miss her early mornings, but she learned many years ago "that my spiritual life isn't contingent on daily devotional time."

This is a good reminder to daily people. A missed day or two doesn't indicate spiritual failure or lead to condemnation from God. Daily people need to give themselves grace when they can't follow their daily spiritual practices.

JASON

Jason, who serves in ministry in Croatia with his wife and three young children, discovered he has a weekly/monthly life rhythm. "It has opened my eyes to a new way of knowing Jesus," Jason says. "I always felt guilty not only about not doing daily devotions but also about not wanting to do them. Discovering that it is okay to spend more time once every few weeks rather than a little bit every day was a huge game changer for me. Now, I get more out of my time with God and don't have this constant dread looming over me every time I look at my Bible."

Jason describes how the new reality of his life rhythm has enhanced his relationship with God. "Since starting this, I find myself praying more frequently at random times during the day, for short periods of time. I don't have the guilt, so I love spending time with him instead of feeling obligated to."

Seeing he can carve out a block of time every few weeks or take one day a month to center on God has been a liberating perspective for Jason. He finds leaving his home for these spiritual intensives works best. He might end up at a coffee shop to read and pray over Scripture, considering what God is saying to his heart. When he desires a more intimate connection, he will hop in his car, drive to a place where he can be alone (sometimes not even leaving the car), and speak out loud, expressing his praise to God.

"The best part about living within my life rhythm is that I love reading the Bible and praying now. That feeling of guilt or failure whenever I look at the Bible by my bed is gone. It is okay that I haven't read it in a week. I have a block of time set aside I can get excited for."

No longer burdened by the dread and angst of feeling obligated to a certain way of doing things, Jason is free to enjoy God within the beat of his natural rhythm.

LISA

Connecting with God outside of our natural rhythm creates a cacophony of tension, effort, and failure. This was Lisa's experience. Lisa, a high school music teacher, describes it this way. "When I first heard of 'Life Rhythm Theory,' it was truly a discovery! My entire life I have been told that 'good' Christians read their Bible every day—in the morning. As a seasonal/yearly person (not to mention a night owl), I tried time and again to be 'good,' and would always fail. This spiritual failure was always looming like a dark shadow on an otherwise vibrant, growing walk with Christ. I felt like I was letting him down."

Perhaps what clued Lisa in to her rhythm was the way she related to the highs and lows a seasonal person experiences. "I felt such a release," she explains, "when I heard some of us go through seasons with God—some times of intense spiritual discovery and growth and other times of what may seem like a drought. It was the first time I ever heard I was designed this way by a God who doesn't expect me to be anyone other than me!"

If you're in a low season, give yourself permission to lean into the dry time, seeing God even when life isn't super productive or highly spiritual.

Lisa also realized her journal entries were sporadic. "I noticed there were periods of daily journal entries during intense times of spiritual revelation and growth. These intense times would be followed by days or weeks or even months of no journal entries."

If you're a seasonal/yearly person, perhaps you'll relate with the following image that Lisa shares: "For me, being seasonal looks like a cross-country road trip. There are legs of the trip spent in the mountains, inevitably followed by a journey into the valley, with stretches of plains in the middle. My journey looks different from those who choose to take a plane or train, but our destination is the same."

Lisa has found freedom to read her Bible at night, and feels "absolutely no guilt if it's not every day." On the other hand, she gives a warning that "we should never use our rhythm as an excuse for not investing in our spiritual growth. No, I am not a daily person. But I should not let my relationship with Christ be put on the back burner."

Lisa is referring to the low times seasonal/yearly people will experience. A dry season can follow a highly productive or intense time of spiritual growth. Recognizing the low time as just that—a low time—gives the seasonal person permission to rest in God's love even though they can't feel, express, or experience the exhilaration of the high times. Besides, if a highly productive time has come to an end, rest may be what is most needed in the next season.

Seasonal/yearly people can be looked upon as lazy, but they have to be comfortable in their own rhythm. Dry times are not bad, by any means. Rather than putting Christ on the back burner, as Lisa puts it, the seasonal person can find ways to connect with God in the low times. Find things that keep you encouraged and refreshed. Perhaps it's a good book to read, or finding something creative that ministers to the body, mind, and spirit. The idea of praying in color that I described in chapter ten can be therapeutic in the low times. It's a way to keep in touch with God in a reflective and creative way.

Seasonal people can be assured there will be an end to the low time, which is good to remember in the middle of such a season. And they can count on a new season that promises productivity and spiritual growth. If you're in a low season, give yourself permission to lean into the dry time, seeing God even when life isn't super productive or highly spiritual. You're not abandoning God. He hasn't abandoned you. He's still there. You're still walking in faith even if it's at a slower pace, and the slower pace doesn't bother God. "I'm so thankful for the closeness I feel to the Lord on the mountain, and the lessons in faith and trust he teaches me in the valley," Lisa says.

Though this book has concentrated on life rhythm as it relates to the spiritual side of life, knowing your life rhythm can also lend perspective to your work. Lisa gained understanding into her profession as a music teacher, realizing there are times when she is disorganized and other times when organization seems to be a priority. "As a creative, big-picture thinker, I struggle with organization. But I have found I have intense times of productivity, mainly the all-school musical I direct, where I become organized and focused . . . probably because I can see the end result, the reason for the productivity." When a seasonal/yearly person sees how something fits into the greater scheme of things, they launch in with a fervor that gets the job done.

BEN AND HEATHER

Ben and Heather, a vibrant young couple engaged in immigrant ministry in Vienna, Austria, found the concept of life rhythm to be not only personally freeing but also revealing for their marriage. Ben falls into the weekly/ monthly life rhythm. Heather sees herself fitting perfectly into the seasonal/yearly rhythm.

Heather is embracing the freedom to find ways that she connects with God instead of forcing herself to "fit into a fifteen-minute daily regimen," a common frustration for the seasonal/yearly person. Blocking out time every day becomes draining and repetitious, plus fifteen minutes a day won't be long enough for the seasonal person.

"As a seasonal person, I have found that I enjoy breaking my Bible study into themes," says Heather. "I will read one or more passages that focus on a specific theme and then incorporate other practices into my life that reflect that theme. My spiritual formation relies heavily on conversing with others about their own experiences, listening to podcasts, reading literature, being in nature, etc."

Ben's discovery of his weekly/monthly rhythm has enabled him to be free to be the best version of himself in how he relates to God. He shares it allows him to "embrace longer periods of focused devotional time a couple times a week," adding that "fifteen to twenty minutes never felt like enough," because he never had the time to really contemplate the Word. Now Ben sets aside a day or two a week to dig deeper into whatever he's studying.

Weekly/monthly people enjoy their Sunday respite from the labors of the week.

Ben now realizes Heather pictures life in seasons, sometimes highly productive, sometimes not. Heather also said, "It seems I experience emotions more deeply and much longer than others." That helps Ben to acknowledge her emotions, accepting and loving her through the season, and affirming her with a listening ear and encouragement. Ben says, "Being aware of our life rhythms helps us to anticipate and create space for each of our needs."

Heather now realizes Ben is more concerned about the end goal than about what happens in a day. He sets alarms or electronic alerts to help him remember events or meetings throughout the week or month. Heather anticipates his need to set aside time within his week or month for deeper study. Though she isn't a calendar girl, she sees the importance of having a bit of a structured plan in order to help Ben prepare for upcoming events.

Discovering life rhythm has helped Ben and Heather enter life and engage with God based on their unique identities. Heather shares, "The more I embrace who I am, the healthier I become and the easier it is for me to connect with God. I am able to shed the feelings of guilt I often carried at my failure to be entirely filled by brief daily devotions, and can now look for the unique ways Jesus meets me where I am. Being comfortable in my own skin allows me to be more available to others."

Ben shares, "I am now able to be entirely comfortable with myself and the way in which my brain works. I can be intentional about taking time and organizing my life in ways that best suit me and help me to live a fuller life."

DUSTIN

Dustin is a fun-loving guy who is in love with his wife and is a great dad to three little ones. He works hard to make a difference in Haiti, the most poverty-stricken country in the Western Hemisphere. His perseverance in a difficult culture may stem from his experience in the military, where he was deployed twice to Iraq.

Dustin had a solid Christian upbringing yet battled with what it meant to be a "good" Christian. He says, "Ignorance is bliss, but not when it comes to my spiritual walk. Growing up in a Christian home and attending church four-plus times a week, you hear the things a 'good' Christian needs to do in order to maintain a close relationship with God." He said he felt he had to have devotions every single morning at the same time or he was failing in his duty as a Christian.

Dustin felt great freedom in his spiritual walk when he realized that being a good Christian had nothing to do with reading the right things at the right time. It was a life-changing day when Dustin realized he was normal in having a seasonal/yearly life rhythm. He no longer had to beat himself up for not having a daily time, though it has been difficult for him to get accustomed to having a seasonal rhythm after so many years of thinking differently.

When his wife, Nancy, heard the life rhythm descriptions, she instantly knew that Dustin was a seasonal person. She said it helped to make more sense in their relationship after discovering Dustin's life rhythm.

The best part of knowing his life rhythm, Dustin shares, is being able to see how he can grow closer in his relationship with Christ. He reports that understanding this rhythm has also had a positive effect on his marriage and personal friendships.

SHEREE

A wife, the mother of three active boys, and the pastor of a church in the mountains of Ecuador, Sheree finds that her weekly/monthly rhythm is her lifeline for replenishment in the midst of a full life. An athlete at heart, Sheree runs two or three times a week to relieve stress and keep in shape.

Discovering her unique life rhythm has given her more freedom to plan chunks of time that work within her schedule. Sheree plans a three-hour time of solitude on Friday afternoons, which she says gives her "more time and room to experience God and to listen to him, versus trying to squeeze in a thirty-minute daily time," which makes her feel pressured and rushed.

On these afternoons, she says, "I disappear from my home, office, work, and ministry to get away with God; to be alone with him, his Word, and his voice." She says, "I journal, I read, I reflect, I listen." She might also take a long prayer walk during the afternoon.

In addition to her Friday afternoon appointments, Sheree plans a monthly day away with God (DAWG) to refresh and restore her soul. She likens these longer times of refreshment to the rest described in Psalm 23 and Matthew 11:28–30. During her DAWG, Sheree is more intentional about practicing silence, stillness, rest, and retreat. She says, "I normally work through some of the 'sacred rhythms'—like confession, self-examination (see Ps. 139:23), discernment, and life check-in outlined in Ruth Haley Barton's books." These chunks of refreshment and renewal are significant for Sheree, so much so that she states, "I guard my Friday afternoon times and my DAWGs with my life . . . Only emergencies interrupt those times because I need them that much!"

Understanding the different life rhythms has helped Sheree "bless others with the freedom and grace to find the rhythm that works best with how God made and shaped them." She adds, "It also helps me not to put others in a box, not to think they have to experience God the same way I do." That includes her husband, an engineer, who likes structure. As a daily person, he needs his daily 5:00 a.m. journal, coffee, and Bible time to orient himself for the day. Sheree concludes that knowing their unique life rhythms "helps us work together to give each other the space and time to experience and follow God in the ways that most naturally beat with our own hearts."

BOB AND MARCIA

Bob, after working as a doctor in the United States for thirty years, is practicing medicine on the Haitian island of La Gonave, sharing his medical expertise at the island's only hospital. Since arriving on the island, he felt the lack of "a strong weekly rhythm," which he'd experienced back home through group worship. Bob says, "Not that I feel distant from God, but I don't have those times of special communion like I did in the past."

Weekly/monthly people enjoy their Sunday respite from the labors of the week. Bob is clearly a weekly/monthly person, even though he continues to have daily quiet times. "I've not been one to be as impacted by personal quiet times as some are. I do it regularly, but it's more of a discipline than a joy most days; not dreary, just a daily discipline." Non-daily people can certainly incorporate daily disciplines into their life, but it won't have as much impact for them as it will the daily person.

It is in weekly worship that Bob finds his most consistent experience of God speaking. He longs to worship "with a group of believers in my native tongue, having a time with them when I can just listen, reflect, sing, kneel, cry." He finds these times of worship touch his emotions, give insight, and create communion with God and others.

Bob's wife, Marcia, gives direction to visiting teams who come to support the hospital and island ministries with their talents and professions. When she lived in the states, Marcia, a daily person, had well-established rhythms. Upon their move to La Gonave, she felt at first that it was best to loosen up on her former patterns in order to be open to her new role and new ways of doing things. But she found she couldn't function in a rhythm outside of her natural beat. "That was probably not the best way for me," she said. "It left me feeling aimless and not well connected."

No matter what our life rhythm, we all desire the same outcome: spiritual growth that transforms us to be more like Jesus.

After several months of trying to fit into an unnatural rhythm, she decided to sit down and "actually write out a day-by-day, hour-by-hour schedule" so she would know what she would be doing from one day to the next—allowing flexibility for a couple of different scenarios. Some weeks in Marcia's new life on the island are busy with visiting teams; other weeks are not.

True to the daily rhythm, Marcia found that mapping her life on a daily basis anchored her in the routines necessary for her to be effective. She says, "I am finding that having a clear expectation for myself is important in my sense of making a worthwhile contribution here."

DINA

Dina, the friend whose bread-making analogy I mentioned in chapter 4, would remember my "survey days," when I asked people when, where, and how they had their daily devotions. I recall Dina giving me the strangest look when I asked her about her personal devotions. Clearly, it didn't matter so much to her, a sign that she wasn't caught up in trying to be something she wasn't. She was already in sync with her natural rhythm as a weekly/monthly person, long before I discovered life rhythms.

Dina lives in Vienna, Austria, with her husband, Dave. Because Dina enjoys the seasons of Advent and Lent, you might think she is a seasonal/yearly person, but she explains these particular holidays help her "to lay out the coming month or the next forty days." She relates, "During Advent last year, I drew an Advent tree. I liked seeing the tree filled in with words to describe the season. It was an easy way for me to include my family too. There were twenty-five circles, but I didn't do one every day. Sometimes I did two or three in a day. I used a daily devotional and Scripture as inspiration for the words."

So even though Dina enjoys connecting with Christian holidays and did a creative project for Advent, that doesn't necessarily mean that she is a seasonal/yearly person. She does admit she finds herself "split between monthly and seasonal," but she usually sees herself as "more task-oriented than process-oriented," a good indication that she probably leans into the weekly/monthly rhythm. The key phrase that distinguishes her as a weekly/monthly person is found in her comment about laying out her weekly/monthly plan. Seasonal people don't usually lay out an intentional plan. They may process a season, and that might even include an Advent calendar, but their process likely won't be as intentional or task oriented as would that of a weekly/monthly person.

Over the years I've seen Dina's weekly/monthly tendency of surrounding herself with a team to set goals, launch new projects, and see them through to completion. And she can manage a number of spinning plates without losing momentum. Dina sums up the best part of living within her life rhythm in one word: *freedom!*

FREEDOM

We each have the freedom to engage with God according to our unique life rhythm. Joy, Jason, Ben, Heather, Lisa, Dustin, Sheree, Bob, Marcia, and Dina have given us glimpses of their spiritual formation in light of their life rhythm. No matter what our life rhythm, we all desire the same outcome: spiritual growth that transforms us to be more like Jesus.

Daily people like Joy and Marcia have the freedom to embrace the consistency and simplicity of routines and daily patterns. While the other rhythms may be a little more complicated, the simplicity of the daily rhythm means it can be sustained for years, or even a lifetime. Daily people don't have to think too much about longer-term goals or give thought to what the next season will bring. They do what they do every day. I recently met a man who has read through the Bible each year for three decades. That's the consistency and steadiness of a daily person. Their discipline is unmatched.

Weekly/monthly people like Jason, Ben, Sheree, Bob, and Dina have the freedom to plan or arrange spiritual practices within larger blocks of time that are meaningful to them. They will be intentional about planning time with God that coordinates with their schedule, and then make sure it happens. Whatever goal or plan is currently at hand will determine what spiritual practices they engage in week by week and month by month. It won't always look the same. Once their growth plan or goals are carried out, the weekly/monthly person will change things up to fit the next spiritual growth pursuit or focus.

Seasonal/yearly people like Heather, Lisa, and Dustin need permission more than a plan. They find freedom by simply giving themselves permission to engage in spiritual practices with flexibility and variety. Exploring new things that offer a fresh perspective on their spiritual walk is a delight to them. The ebb and flow of life will often determine their spiritual focus and practices for each season.

Discovering life rhythm sets people free to enter a deeper communion with God, embracing his love without condemnation or guilt. Old spiritual practices take on new meaning when incorporated into one's life rhythm. When we think of spiritual practices, prayer and Bible reading are usually the first things that come to mind. Though these are two primary avenues for connecting with God, there are many more. In the next chapter, we'll take a closer look at these spiritual practices and how they can enhance your relationship with God as you connect according to your life rhythm.

PERSONAL REFLECTION

1. Of the ten people who described their life rhythm in this chapter, which one did you identify with the most, and why?

2. What new insights into your life rhythm did you gain while reading this chapter?

3. If you were to describe your discovery of a personal life rhythm in one word, what would it be, and why?

ENGAGING THE SPIRITUAL PRACTICES

part 4

12

THE HEARTBEAT OF SPIRITUAL FORMATION

why we do what we do

Spiritual formation is for everyone. Just as there is an 'outer you' that is being formed and shaped all the time, like it or not, by accident or on purpose, so there is an 'inner you.' You have a spirit. And it's constantly being shaped and tugged at: by what you hear and watch and say and read and think and experience.

–John Ortberg

One day, while writing a reflection paper for a spiritual formation class I was taking toward ordination, the Holy Spirit spoke to me, mid-sentence. Sitting there at my desk at home, tears filled my eyes, and I put my hand over my mouth, taken aback by the thought that came to my mind: *I was making personal devotions an idol.*

Keith Drury's *With Unveiled Faces* was one of the textbooks for the class. In it, he describes various spiritual practices, but the impact point for me that day came in his conclusion: "If we believe the disciplines themselves make us holy, we have made an idol of them. . . . When we do this, we are actually relying on *ourselves*—on *our* discipline—to become holy."[1]

The spiritual practices are not an end in themselves, nor are they a means to an end. They do not make us holy, nor do they promise to bring about maturity. It's not the practices that matter so much as having a heart that opens itself to hear from God. It's the Holy Spirit who grows us, renews us, and transforms us, not the practices.

God's Word is powerful, but it isn't God. He uses it to reveal himself and speak to us. Prayer is significant, but prayer isn't God. It's an avenue by which we can have a conversation with him. I believe in the power of fasting, but fasting isn't God. It's a time period set aside to focus on him and attune ourselves to his Spirit in a deeper way. We may love to express our thoughts through journaling, but journaling isn't God. He establishes our thoughts as we write and draws us to him as we consider his ways. Solitude is not God. The quietness allows us to be free of distractions so we can center on him.

In that moment of revelation in my study, I realized all these practices simply put me in a place where I am apt to connect with God. I had been so focused on the wrong thing, the practices themselves, rather than the God to whom they point. Richard Foster expresses these same thoughts in his book *Celebration of Discipline*. "[Disciplines] are not the answer; they only lead us to the Answer. We must clearly understand this limitation of the disciplines if we are to avoid bondage."[2] When we engage in spiritual practices outside of our life rhythm, they may very well become the cause of spiritual bondage. Wouldn't it be like the enemy of our souls to take the gifts that God has given for our spiritual growth and distort them to the point of becoming a burden that brings discouragement and defeat?

It's bad enough when the spiritual practices become a source of pride, as they did for the religious leaders of Jesus' day. It's even worse when we begin with a vital life in Jesus but strive to fit into a rhythm not our own, experiencing defeat and failure. Remember Lisa in the previous chapter, whose rhythm was seasonal/yearly? You may recall that trying to force herself into a daily rhythm resulted in what she described as "spiritual failure" that "was always looming, like a dark shadow on an otherwise vibrant, growing walk with Christ." If you've been using spiritual practices outside the natural beat of your life rhythm, you're probably a frustrated, sometimes defeated, believer. That can change as you learn to engage in spiritual practices in keeping with your life rhythm. But before that happens, it's important to realize two things. First, you'll need to understand spiritual formation and its purpose. Second, you'll need to gain an idea of why we engage in spiritual practices. Then you'll be in a position to explore the practices and use them to aid your spiritual growth.

UNDERSTANDING SPIRITUAL FORMATION

Spiritual formation has become a buzzword, and we may question whether the term itself continues to have value. I am confident that it does. Spiritual formation is best defined by these four essential elements: life change, engaging in community, participation in the Spirit's work, and love for others. Let's examine each one.

life change

Our approach to God will vary according to our personality, background, experiences, stage of life, and, yes, life rhythm. The Spirit weaves the individual characteristics God has given us together with our life influences and experiences to form Christ in us. When we believe there is only one way to proceed spiritually, we miss the variety of practices that align us with God, we are unaware of how our uniqueness relates with our spiritual growth, and we live with a skewed understanding of the nature of God. In short, we miss out on the abundant life promised in Jesus. One reason we fall into that trap is we make the mistake of seeing spiritual practices as an end in themselves. This was the problem I realized in myself while writing that paper on spiritual formation.

The purpose of spiritual formation is not to engage in spiritual practices. It is to have Christ formed in us. So the best measure of our spiritual growth is not that we engage in spiritual practices; it is where those practices lead us. Do they change us? Do they produce Christ's character in us? Do they make a difference in how we love others? This is the heartbeat of spiritual formation. It's not about what we *do* to draw closer to God. It's about *being* like Jesus. Yet even that idea does not fully express the goal of spiritual formation, for it is never about us alone. It is always for the sake of others.

community

Robert Mulholland, in his book *Invitation to a Journey*, reminds us that the believer is "conformed to the image of Christ for the sake of others *within* the body of Christ and for the sake of others *outside* the body of Christ."[3] Mulholland's words allow a liberating shift from the mind-set that the spiritual practices exist solely for one's own personal growth and holiness. In that mind-set, the extreme is to become "judgmental, self-righteous persons who look down their pious noses at the world in its brokenness and bondage."[4]

Unfortunately, this is often how Christians are viewed today. Our focus on personal holiness has turned us inward. We are personally pious but outwardly condemning, having too little love and care for the broken people around us. I call this lopsided Christianity. Our faith can never be just about us and our love for God; it has to include loving others in the spirit of Jesus. To emphasize personal holiness without social holiness is to end up without any holiness at all. Spiritual practices can help us to grow in knowledge and in relationship with God, but if they're used as the sole measurement of our spirituality, then we have missed what spiritual formation is about. God's transforming power becomes evident in us only when it results in demonstrating his love to others.

engaging with the spirit

The apostle Paul defined spiritual formation when he spoke of his longing and desire to see the believers in Galatia having Christ "formed in" them (Gal. 4:19 NIV). What does it mean to have Christ formed in me? In you? Let's take a look at each word.

Christ. It's about Jesus and his character, which is love.

Formed. It is to be developed, molded, and shaped. It is Jesus' character taking shape in our lives from the inside out, his character emerging in a way that is visible to others.

In. It's Jesus' Spirit within us, down to the core of our inner being. It's who we are—heart, mind, and soul.

You. It includes us—our unique personalities, strengths, passions, longings, desires, gifts, talents, and life experiences—all transformed and empowered by the Holy Spirit both for our sake and for the sake of others.

This means that spiritual formation is an intensely personal and active process. Our lives are a little more complicated than a tree or a flower, but even these simple elements of nature give glory to God by being precisely what they were made to be. The Scriptures speak of this. Hills sing. Rivers clap. The sea shouts. Trees and fields clap their hands. The heavens give God glory—the sun, the moon, and the stars. If you're like me, you can see and feel the majesty of our creator God in nature.

If such lowly objects give glory to God in unique ways, then certainly human beings can give glory to God by being ourselves—by being precisely who we were made to be. Embracing our life rhythm is part of being ourselves, which brings glory to God simply because it's how he created us. It's also how we can be most effective and find the most freedom to engage with God.

Working with God to discover our true selves is a lifetime journey as we see and understand the work God is doing *in* us (see 1 Thess. 5:23–24). The other side of this is a lifetime commitment to see and understand the work

God is doing *through* us—for the sake of others (2:8). If we reject this thought, we dismiss the very reason we exist in this life at all. Christ is formed in you to

- embrace the life God has given you within his will and love;
- discover who you are in light of his truth and love; and
- participate in God's love for others.

Understanding your life rhythm simply enables you to engage with God in the flow of your unique rhythm, whether you're daily, weekly/monthly, or seasonal/yearly. What really matters in your spiritual formation is this: Is Christ being formed in you? And is his Spirit within you evident to others (see Gal. 5:22–23)?

love for others

Dallas Willard says, "the aim and substance of spiritual life" is not what we often think it is.[5] It's not how long or how often I read the Bible. It's not when or where I pray, or the length of my prayer time. It's not about which fast I choose or how long I fast. Though meeting together with believers is important, the essence of the spiritual life is not even how regularly I attend church. It is, according to Willard, "the effective and full enjoyment of active love of God and humankind in all the daily rounds of normal existence where we are placed."[6] This is how Jesus lived.

Willard points out that Jesus "showed us that spiritual strength is not manifested by great and extensive practice of the spiritual disciplines, but by little need to practice them and still maintain full spiritual life." He further suggests "the spiritually advanced person is not the one who engages in lots and lots of disciplines, any more than the good child is the one who receives lots and lots of instruction and punishment."[7] Willard goes even further, implying that strict, self-disciplined abstinence like that of the desert fathers—placing a high emphasis on spiritual practices as the standard and measurement of Christianity—was the "fundamental and devastating error of Christian asceticism in the Western church."[8] There is an ascetic side to connecting with God, but perhaps the church unintentionally emphasized personal reflection and solitude as the only way to meet with God.

If the spiritual practices are not effective in producing the intended result—Christ formed in us—then what good are they doing? If we are not fully enjoying the active love of God in our lives, what has become of the relationship the practices are supposed to be nurturing? If we are not manifesting the fruit of the Spirit in the daily, weekly, monthly, or seasonal rounds of life, then what difference do the spiritual practices make in how we live and do life? So if your spiritual practices are not drawing you to God and helping to form Christ in you, then stop doing them. Instead, find out what helps Christ take shape in you, empowering you to actively love others like Jesus did.

We know Jesus engaged in spiritual practices, such as going away to quiet places, spending all night in prayer, and taking time to rest. Yet these practices are not the focus of the gospel writers. The stories that fill the pages of the Gospels tell us more about how Jesus loved and showed compassion than about his spiritual practices. He offered healing, extended forgiveness, and cared for the poor. Most of Jesus' teachings and parables were about God's generous love and forgiveness. The stories about Jesus tell us how he loved.

Loving others in the spirit of Jesus may be the most significant of all spiritual practices. Without love of others, the spiritual practices have no value. That may be difficult for some to hear, but living for God is so much more than spiritual practices. Many of us have made the spiritual practices themselves the measurement of our spirituality, so much so that some don't know how to have a spiritual life apart from the practices.

PERSONAL REFLECTION

1. Consider Keith Drury's words, "If we believe the disciplines themselves make us holy, we have made an idol of them." Take time to quietly listen. Ask God where your dependence lies in your journey to become holy. Is it on your own merit or on God's love, grace, and transforming power?

2. In what ways do you measure your spirituality?

3. Take time to examine your own heart. What is your experience of the spiritual practices? If need be, confess you've made them an idol, renounce the lie that the disciplines make you holy, and declare the truth that God is the only one who makes you holy.

13

FOLLOW HIS LEAD

choosing spiritual practices
for your life rhythm

The Disciplines allow us to place ourselves before
God so that he can transform us.

—Richard Foster

When I introduce the concept of life rhythms in workshops, invariably someone approaches me with this question, "Now that I know my life rhythm, how does it fit into my spiritual growth?" I would venture to say that most people who ask this are thinking of how to engage in spiritual practices, not of the outcome. They're really asking, "How do I *do* this?" not "What does life in the Spirit look like?" I don't say this condescendingly; it merely shows how fully we have been misinformed about the reason for the spiritual practices.

I am hesitant to offer a plan for—or even examples of—what spiritual practices might look like in a particular life rhythm. My hesitancy stems from two things. First, I realize that I'm writing as a seasonal/yearly person. Plan? What plan? As a seasonal/yearly person, having a plan freaks me out. I don't wish to impose that anxiety on other seasonal folks by suggesting how they should engage in spiritual practices.

The second reason I hesitate to suggest a plan is by suggesting how another person should engage in spiritual formation, I may cause them to be locked into a certain way of doing things. That could lead them right back to where we started—feeling guilty and defeated because they can't measure up to the model others think they should follow. In his book, *Spirituality for the Rest of Us*, Larry Osborne calls it "best practices overload," when we try to imitate what everybody else is doing.[1] I hesitate to offer plans for engaging with spiritual practices because I don't want others to miss the point of spiritual formation and be untrue to themselves.

Yet I realize while there are many resources available to the daily person, there is very little, if anything, available to help those who follow a weekly/monthly or seasonal/yearly life rhythm. It would be dishonoring to others and to God to hold back helpful elements that could be life giving. I'm writing this book to share the freedom of discovering life rhythm, not to leave others hanging in limbo. I trust the cautions and misunderstandings that I've addressed will help to keep the practices in their proper place.

using life-change questions

Perhaps the best way to answer the question "How does my spiritual growth fit into my life rhythm?" is to prayerfully ask some further questions. These questions explore the four essential elements of spiritual formation—life change, engaging in community, participating with the Holy Spirit's work in our lives, and actively loving others. No matter which life rhythm you lean into, the questions fit because they're not about the practices. Instead they are about growth, life change, and living a full life in Christ.

Where is God leading me to change? Perhaps it's an area that needs to be reshaped or retooled. Perhaps it's an area that needs to be renewed or refreshed. Maybe it's a roadblock to reaching deeper wisdom or maturity.

- Is there a new revelation of his character or a new sense of his love for me that I need to embrace?
- Is there a truth I need to face in order to open myself up to the full life that Jesus promised?
- Is there a point of bondage in my life? Bondage is indicated by a repeated cycle of sin and confession, as Paul describes in Romans 7:14–25.
- Is there a new level of freedom I can obtain?
- Is anything negatively affecting my physical or emotional health?
- What might be harming my relationships?
- Is there a sin that hinders my relationship with God?
- Is there part of my past that's holding me back that I could address through redemptive remembering?
- Is there a dimension of my life controlled by fear instead of love?

- Would the development of a certain fruit of the Spirit (see Gal. 5:22–23) produce Christlikeness in me and in my relationships?

Who can join or help me in growing spiritually? The second question deals with community. Who can come alongside me to encourage and affirm what God is doing in and through my life? This might be a friend or friends, a counselor, spiritual director, life coach, accountability partner, a small group, or a spiritually mature mentor.

What practices and tools can assist in my growth? The third question centers on our activity in spiritual formation, in keeping with our unique identity. What spiritual practices or specific tools will help me to participate with the Holy Spirit's work in my life?

What opportunities do I have to demonstrate God's love to others? The fourth question leads us to examine our love for others. Where is God's love being demonstrated in the context where God has placed me—where I live and do life with others?

- Is there a particular person whom I can specifically reach out to in love?
- Do I actively seek to follow God's prompting to discern an opportunity to act in someone's life?
- Do I listen, really hearing the heart of another's story?
- Am I creating space for God in my conversations?
- What would **love** have me do today, this week, this month, this season, or this year?

Whatever your life rhythm, these questions will enable you to be intentional about your spiritual growth. Rather than creating a plan, consider using these questions as a guide in determining how God is leading you. The questions are not meant to be an exhaustive list of possibilities but to provide a jump-start on your journey to Christlikeness.

Though only one question specifically mentions spiritual practices, all the questions deal with your spiritual formation. The specific spiritual practices you eventually choose will be guided by your answers to these questions. The questions will help you gain wisdom and spiritual understanding (see Col. 1:9), and align your heart with God. All the questions pertain to God's active involvement in your life to make you more like him. God is not only interested in your spiritual life; he is interested in the rest of your life as well.

keeping the focus on wholeness

We have seen that spiritual practices are intended to support our spiritual formation—Christ formed in us. So choosing practices is not as simple as mapping out a template. We choose them with our individual growth needs in mind. A related idea is we must choose spiritual practices with an eye toward our entire being. The practices are not intended to affect only the spiritual area of life; they must impact every area of our being.

I was discussing my life verse with a friend who is a spiritual director and also trains others in spiritual direction. I had claimed Colossians 1:28–29 (NIV) years ago, as the verse that represented my lifelong mission: "He is the one we proclaim, admonishing and teaching everyone with all wisdom, so that we may present everyone fully mature in Christ. To this end I strenuously contend with all the energy Christ so powerfully works in me." This passage of Scripture blended my God-given gifts, strengths, and passions to come along side believers in their growth in Christ. My friend pondered out loud, "What if grace was God responding to us because he sees us whole and wants us to experience that wholeness?"

My friend's insight made sense. Sometimes I have to remind myself that I am a whole person. God made me as an intellectual, physical, emotional, and spiritual being. He takes interest in all of me. If one aspect of my being is affected by something, the rest of my being feels it.

Christ formed in me means Christ formed in *all* of me. He transforms every aspect of my being and uses all of me to make a difference where he has placed me in the world. The same is true for you. God had great hope for us before the world even began. Before you and I were born, he loved us. Just like parents anticipating a newborn baby, God had loving thoughts of you and me before we existed. But he also knew what was to come. He knew about the ugly invasion of sin and its destruction in the world. He knew what that would mean for us. We needed to be rescued from the curse of sin and death. And so, long ago, "even before he made the world," God had a plan (Eph. 1:4 NLT).

I can only imagine the anticipation and enthusiasm God had when planning the redemption of mankind. It was a plan birthed out of his sovereignty, wisdom, and understanding, combined with a love and kindness this world may never fully understand. It is a plan that still

I CAN ONLY
IMAGINE THE
ANTICIPATION
AND ENTHUSIASM
GOD HAD WHEN
PLANNING THE
REDEMPTION
OF MANKIND.

stands today. And God's plan for redemption pictured us whole. Though we were born spiritually dead due to sin, God, through Christ's death and resurrection, enables our spirit to live, to be alive in Christ forever. Salvation begins in a miraculous moment of becoming spiritually alive. No wonder Jesus said the heavens would rejoice when one person repents (Luke 15:7). That we be made wholly alive in Christ is what he intended all along.

When you respond to his hope and love for you, the spirit part of your being comes alive, and that will affect all the other parts of who you are. Wholeness in Christ will impact your attitude, your behavior, your thoughts, your relationships, your desires, and your heart. God desires us whole and wants us to experience wholeness. It's important to keep this in mind as we take a closer look at the spiritual practices.

using practices versus disciplines

I usually refer to the spiritual disciplines as spiritual practices. Maybe it's because I'm a seasonal/yearly person. Discipline only lasts for so long before a new season turns over and it's time to change things up. I trust those who fall into the other two life rhythms, who may like the word *disciplines*, will bear with my verbiage.

My take on the word *discipline* is some spiritual practices may require discipline if the practice does not come naturally to the individual. Scripture memorization may not come easily, but one can commit to doing it with the knowledge that a constructive verse can be beneficial both in providing encouragement and in bringing about change. We may not enjoy solitude, but detaching from life and people for a time helps us to focus on things pertinent to our spiritual growth, like heart examination, reflection, confession, and prayer. It may be some practices take discipline because they don't come easily, but are still necessary toward spiritual growth for a time. Jesus fasted for forty days in the desert in preparation for the coming years of ministry. He spent all night in prayer before selecting the twelve disciples. Self-control may be in order when a particular practice diverges from the natural pattern of life, or when it is the opposite of our personality.

Nate, who was the youth pastor in one church Dennis and I served, is one of the most expressive people I know. A lover of people, he laughs easily, likes to tease, and raises up others who love to serve alongside him. Nate is a fun, loving dad to four beautiful children. On one occasion, my husband and I were joining others from our church at a movie theater. As soon as we entered the lobby, Nate made a run for Dennis, picked him up with both arms, and began to spin him around while proclaiming to moviegoers, "This is my pastor! This is my pastor!" That's Nate.

Now imagine Nate in a small, quiet, prayer room. All by himself.

During my first year overseeing the prayer ministry of the church, we created a prayer room with stations that gave specific instructions on ways to pray. Nate signed up to pray in the room for an hour. I happened to be nearby when Nate exited the prayer room. He was shaking his head and wiping his brow. "I just about went crazy in there," he told me. Solitude—the practice of abstaining from companionship and interaction—is not Nate's strong suit, nor will it be a way he naturally connects with God. If Nate senses God leading him to spend time in solitude, it will take discipline to obey.

As God leads, you may choose a practice that takes discipline, but most likely you will enter into practices that align with your temperament, unique gifts, and passions. I enjoy writing and reflection, so journaling is a practice that I have kept up over the years, though it isn't daily and isn't always weekly. Digging into the Scriptures with a commentary as my companion feeds my desire for curiosity and depth.

At times God leads me to fast for a season, choosing a day in the week that works best with my schedule. It takes discipline, but I know it's something I need for that time. Some practices will come naturally; others will take discipline. The key is to follow God's lead in which tools you choose.

Now you understand the essential elements of spiritual formation, realize the purpose behind spiritual practices, and have had some orientation on selecting the particular spiritual practices that will help you grow—either on an ongoing basis or for a particular season—we can look more closely at the practices themselves.

THE SPIRITUAL PRACTICES

Most people think of prayer, Bible reading, and fasting as spiritual practices, and those probably are the most commonly used. However, there are many others, maybe more than you realized. Entire books have been written for the purpose of defining these practices, so we won't be exhaustive in describing them here. I simply want to show you some of the many tools available to you.

In his book *With Unveiled Faces*, Keith Drury gives a fresh angle on the spiritual practices: "When we practice the spiritual disciplines we put ourselves in the current of God's river of grace."[2] God's grace is available to us, always flowing. His Spirit will lead regarding how, when, and where to step into the current. Drury groups these channels of grace into three categories. (For a more detailed description of these practices, see Appendix A.)

DISCIPLINES OF ABSTINENCE

FASTING, SILENCE, SOLITUDE, SIMPLICITY, REST, AND SECRECY

DISCIPLINES OF ACTION

JOURNALING, HOSPITALITY, CONFESSION, SCRIPTURE, CHARITY, PRAYER, AND PENANCE

DISCIPLINE OF RESPONSE

RESPONSE

You may already engage in one or two of the practices that Drury lists. Perhaps you discovered a few new practices in the list. The practice of *response* may be a new idea to you. How we respond to life circumstances, especially difficult ones, will be a test of our faith and character. According to James 1:2–4, trials can be one of the most character-building times in life.

In *Spiritual Disciplines for Ordinary People*, Keith Drury names what he calls "disciplines of obedient living." Perhaps you will be surprised at this list of spiritual practices, but they can form Christ in us as much as the more contemplative, quieter practices. You may be engaged in some of these, having never considered the fact they can help form Christ in you. Drury refers to these practices as "lesser known disciplines" of holy living.[3]

INNER PERSONAL PRACTICES

HUMILITY:	PUTTING OFF PRIDE
AMBITIONS:	ABANDONING SELFISH AMBITION
GRUDGES:	FORGIVING OLD HURTS
THOUGHT LIFE:	OVERCOMING IMPURE THOUGHTS

INTERPERSONAL PRACTICES

RESTITUTION:	MAKING THINGS RIGHT
HONESTY:	SPEAKING ABSOLUTE TRUTH
PEACEMAKING:	MENDING BROKEN RELATIONSHIPS
RESTORATION:	RESTORING A FALLEN CHRISTIAN

You might choose one of the practices of abstinence, action, or response as a companion tool to one of the practices of obedience. Scripture can support your use of the practices of obedience. You will find it helpful, for example, to find Scripture that speaks of honesty, forgiving others, or having humility as you engage in those practices. The Scriptures can have an empowering effect on us. "Every part of Scripture is God-breathed and useful one way or another—showing us truth, exposing our rebellion, correcting our mistakes, training us to live God's way. Through the Word we are put together and shaped up for the tasks God has for us" (2 Tim. 3:16–17).

The practices of obedience will most likely include a time of confession, acknowledging before God an area where we have allowed a sinful attitude or pattern to take control of our heart and mind. Practicing restoration will necessarily involve us in community, giving encouragement, prayer support, and practical guidance. Others can be a part of the healing process, for James encouraged us, "Confess your sins to each other and pray for each other so that you can live together whole and healed" (James 5:16). You might also accompany these practices of obedience with fasting, which can have a centering effect on what God is currently doing in your life. Of course, praying about any of these practices will keep you aligned with God's heart as you seek his empowerment for inner life change.

choosing the right tool

I hope you are seeing the ways that spiritual practices can be used as tools to enhance spiritual growth. Doing the practices for the sake of doing them won't amount to anything. They must be joined with the Holy Spirit's work in your life.

The spiritual practices can take on different forms. Some are for individuals; others are for communities or can include other people. Each of the practices can be beneficial for spiritual growth, according to how God leads you. The spiritual practices are opportunities to place ourselves in the pathway of God, in the flow of his grace.

Remember that, as Larry Osborne puts it, spiritual practices are "tools, not rules." He further explains, "As powerful as they can be, tools have no value in themselves. Their value is in what they produce."[4] That's important to keep in mind as you sort through the questions listed earlier to determine what God is doing in your life. Choose the right tool according to how God is leading you, and then build it into your life rhythm.

Years ago, my father-in-law, a carpenter, helped Dennis and me renovate an 1860 farmhouse, the first home we owned. We used heavy-duty sandpaper to grind off old paint on a pine floor. But when it came time to finish the job, we used a different weight of sandpaper to create smooth, polished floors. When adding a deck to the back of our home, my father-in-law rounded up our kids, gave them each a hammer, and taught them how to hammer nails to attach the planks to the deck. There's a difference between a Phillips screwdriver and a slotted screwdriver. Each tool is task specific. When choosing your spiritual tools, prayerfully ask which ones make sense in light of what God is currently doing in your life.

fitting practices into your life rhythm

The wide variety of practices will be inviting to a seasonal/yearly person. If you like to have a defined start and finish to something, you will enjoy trying various practices and changing things up in order to keep things fresh. In the ebb and flow of life, you'll see God in the backdrop of the season or year you find yourself in. Processing life, alone and with others, will give understanding and direction to your spiritual journey.

If you're a daily person, you might choose a smaller number of practices that you stick with for years, or even a lifetime. You'll find freedom in a routine that nourishes your soul in ever-changing ways, yet stays consistent and familiar. The spiritual practices will be the guiding light that sets your course for the day. You'll see God in the steady, consistent beat of your daily rhythm, giving you purpose and clarity for each passing day.

If you're a weekly/monthly person, you'll like the fact you have choices, selecting the right tools for your current spiritual goals and fitting them into your calendar. Living intentionally, you'll see God in the spiritual growth that results from your purposeful activity over the weeks and months. You'll be encouraged and motivated by the progress you see in yourself and others.

following God's lead

Several years ago, while we were in pastoral ministry, Dennis took a three-month sabbatical for renewal and refreshment. Rather than a simple tune-up, he felt he needed a major overhaul. As a weekly/monthly person would do, he mapped out his agenda on the calendar.

He planned a 101-day experience, a sabbatical journey in three segments, each a month long. He built in times when he was completely alone, and times when I joined him.

Dennis carefully thought out ways to enhance these three segments for maximum effectiveness. One of the activities he considered was reading the entire Bible, but he sensed the Holy Spirit saying "no." Perhaps the New Testament? Again, a "no" from the Spirit. As the sabbatical time drew near, Dennis sensed God telling him to read the Twenty-Third Psalm. "But I know that psalm well," was Dennis' first response. But he felt compelled to obey this leading. On the first day of his sabbatical, Dennis opened his Bible and began reading Psalm 23. At verse three, he knew the Spirit had said, "Enough." So Dennis read the first half of the psalm a few more times, remembering insights he had gained and often shared with others. The next day, he read it again. Once again, he felt the same nudge as the day before. He ended at verse three.

"Can this be all I'm going to read for 101 days?" Dennis wondered. He thought of the conversations that would ensue when someone asked, "So, what did you read on your sabbatical?"

He'd say, "Well, I was able to read three verses from one of the best-known chapters in the Bible."

Even so, Dennis never went past Psalm 23. In fact, he never went beyond the first three verses during the entire 101 days. So much for setting goals. God had something else in mind. He wanted the words "The LORD is my shepherd, I have all that I need" (NLT) to sink in deeply. God knew exactly what Dennis needed to refresh his soul. As the sabbatical journey continued, Dennis dwelled on those verses, hearing simple, powerful words from the Shepherd: *Receive my love. Follow my lead.* Dennis, ever the planner, had clearly stepped into God's plan for the sabbatical by responding to the leading of the Shepherd. Of all the experiences in the sabbatical journey—hiking, traveling, reading, meeting with mentors—nothing was as significant as the simple phrase impressed upon a well-led heart. *Receive my love. Follow my lead.* Since then, these words from the Shepherd have been assuring, comforting, and restorative for both of us.

These, too, are wise words to take with us as we consider our life rhythm and how it relates to spiritual formation. Know that God loves you. Know that he desires to lead you. He is not one to push or force. He leads and guides. He is not one to overwhelm with high expectations that drain, defeat, and discourage. He gives rest to those who are wearied by *ought* and *should.* Enjoying his companionship—embracing his love, watching how he loves others—is the best way to learn the unforced rhythms of his grace. His grace gives freedom to live within the beat of a life rhythm that is natural, fulfilling, and life giving. And it is in this place that you will find rest for your soul.

LIVING LIGHTLY

I love the fact that Jesus allows us to experience his unforced rhythms of grace. The goal through all of this is to be loved by him. He invites us to learn his ways, to come and walk with him. The author of Proverbs captures this well. "Trust in the LORD with all your heart; do not depend on your own understanding. Seek his will in all you do, and he will show you which path to take" (Prov. 3:5–6 NLT). It's a reminder that, to the very end, our choice is to follow his lead. Following will always involve trust. Trust is always about relationship. That is the invitation he extends to us, to enter into a trust relationship with him. So in the end, it's about who he is and following his lead.

Listen for his voice. Draw close. Trust. Learn. Be led. Find rest in him. Live freely and lightly.

> Are you tired? Worn out? Burned out on religion? Come to me. Get away with me and you'll recover your life. I'll show you how to take a real rest. Walk with me and work with me—watch how I do it. *Learn the unforced rhythms of grace.* I won't lay anything heavy or ill-fitting on you. Keep company with me and you'll learn to live freely and lightly.
> —Matt. 11:28–30, emphasis added

PERSONAL REFLECTION

1. In your own words, write out what "Christ formed in you" means to you.

2. Consider the four life-changing questions listed in this chapter (and the related questions included with them). Which ones stand out to you? Why?

3. How might you spend time with God differently as a result of reading this book?

4. Share with a friend two new discoveries that have been helpful in your God-connection as a result of reading *Unforced Rhythms*.

SPIRITUAL DISCIPLINES

as listed by Keith Drury in *With Unveiled Faces*

DISCIPLINES OF ABSTINENCE

Fasting—Abstaining from food for a time in order to gain mastery of the physical realm and open us up to the spiritual.

Silence—Abstaining from sound in order to open our spiritual ears and listen more closely to the voice of God.

Solitude—Abstaining from contact with people in order to be alone with God and draw closer to him.

Simplicity—Intentionally paring down our lifestyle to the essentials to free ourselves from the tyranny of things and focus more on spiritual life.

Rest—Retreat from the frantic pace of life in order to be restored physically and spiritually.

Secrecy—Abstaining from taking credit for the good deeds we do.

DISCIPLINES OF ACTION

Journaling—Communing and communicating with God through writing.

Hospitality—Opening our homes, our hearts, and our lives to others in order to develop loving relationships for the glory of God.

Confession—Humbly admitting our sins and shortcomings to another person as a means of spiritual healing.

Scripture—Reading, studying, memorizing, meditating upon, and obeying the Bible in order to know God and become more like him.

Charity—Giving aid to the poor, motivated by selfless love.

Prayer—A conversation with God through which we come to know him better and develop greater reliance on him.

Penance—Willfully embracing earthly punishment for wrongdoing that has already been forgiven by God.

DISCIPLINE OF RESPONSE

Response—Managing our reactions to what life brings us—both good and bad.

APPENDIX B

GROUP INTERACTION

This practical study on life rhythms will challenge participants to examine their lives through the lens of Scripture and to develop their own personal style of connecting with God. This guide can be used to promote discussion for further learning and understanding of personal life rhythms.

chapter 1

    1. Share your salvation experience and spiritual journey.

    2. What elements of your spiritual upbringing so guided your life you still live by them?

    3. Identify any aspect of your Christian journey that became an *ought* or *should* in your walk with Christ, an element that feels more legalistic than genuine.

chapter 2

1. On a scale from 1 to 10, mark where you currently see your Christian walk. Share why you see yourself in this place.

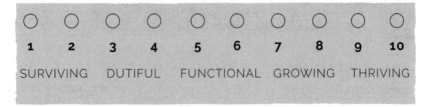

1	2	3	4	5	6	7	8	9	10
SURVIVING		DUTIFUL		FUNCTIONAL		GROWING		THRIVING	

2. In groups of two or three, share the area(s) in your Christian life where you don't feel you measure up.

3. Recall and share a time when you experienced a special awareness of God's presence.

chapter 3

1. Share your personal practices of "time with God."

2. In groups of two or three, share how you view the devotional life—is it a way to gain favor with God or a way to participate with God in what he is doing in your life?

3. Give three reasons why you desire to spend time with God.

chapter 4

1. Share which trail you would have chosen—Pleasing God or Trusting God—before you read this chapter, and why.

2. Split into two groups. Have one group list the reasons for pleasing God and the other list the reasons for trusting God. Take time to share the lists.

3. List characteristics of God that give us reason to trust him.

chapter 5

1. Take time to think about what counts in your Christian life. Is it the spiritual exercises you do, or is it how you live and love others? Share within the group setting.

2. Did the Spirit convict you of ways you might have an attitude like that of the Pharisees? Split into pairs. Share those areas where you struggle with a pharisaical mind-set.

3. Now gather in groups of three. Share practical ways you can express your faith in love. Then come together and share your ideas with the whole group.

4. Discuss your thoughts on the concept of the dark night of the soul. Has anyone ever experienced such a season in life? If so, share how God changed your character as a result of a dark night.

chapter 6

1. Read Matthew 11:28–30 in three different translations or paraphrases. Suggested reading: New International Version, New Living Translation, and The Message. Discuss how the concept of a "yoke of oppression" changes your perspective on this passage.

2. Read the four questions from Barclay to evaluate your spiritual practices. Pair up and share how you answer the questions from your own experience.

3. Consider the difference between loyalty and love. Why isn't loyalty enough in a relationship with Jesus? What difference does love make?

4. Jesus said, "Take my yoke upon you, and learn from me." If the yoke he asks us to carry is the yoke of love, in what ways can we learn how to love from him?

chapter 7

1. Have a different person read each of the "Life Rhythm Theory" descriptions. At the end of each reading, ask which people in the group identify with the one just read. Then create three groups of people sorted by the life rhythm they lean into.

2. In each group, have members share which words or phrases stood out to them in description of the life rhythms.

3. In each group, share how the concept of "Life Rhythm Theory" can change how you approach spiritual practices, or how you view other people's spiritual practices.

chapter 8

1. Have those who identify with a daily rhythm share why they see themselves aligning with this life rhythm.

2. Discuss how knowing someone who lives by a daily rhythm gives a person insight into themselves and others.

chapter 9

1. Have those who identify with a weekly/monthly rhythm share why they see themselves aligning with this life rhythm.

2. Discuss how knowing someone who lives by a weekly/monthly rhythm gives a person insight into themselves and others.

chapter 10

1. Have those who identify with a seasonal/yearly rhythm share why they see themselves aligning with this life rhythm.

2. Discuss how knowing someone who lives by a seasonal/yearly rhythm gives a person insight into themselves and others.

chapter 11

1. Have individuals share which person they related to most strongly in this chapter, and why.

2. In groups of four, talk about how the discovery of life rhythm can strengthen a marriage or friendship.

3. As a group, share in one word what the discovery of life rhythm means to you.

chapter 12

1. Reflect on the idea that disciplines can become an idol. What constitutes an idol?

2. In groups of three, consider the four elements of spiritual formation. Were there any new insights that came from the descriptions of these essential elements?

3. Discuss the idea of lopsided Christianity as defined in this chapter. Do you see this in the world today? Do you see this in your own life? In your church?

chapter 13

1. Quietly read through the life-change questions listed in this chapter (and the related questions). Are there any that speak louder than the others? Connect in pairs and share which questions were highlighted for you. Why?

2. Consider the following: "The practices are not intended to affect only the spiritual area of life; they must impact every area of our being." Is this a new thought

for you and why? Take time for individuals to share in the large group setting.

3. Overall, share how you might spend time with God differently as a result of reading this book.

4. In pairs, share two new discoveries that have been beneficial in connecting with God as a result of reading *Unforced Rhythms*.

NOTES

Introduction

1. Utilizing the online strengths assessment provided by StrengthsFinder has been one of the most defining elements for my life. Marcus Buckingham and Donald O. Clifton, *Now, Discover Your Strengths* (New York: The Free Press, 2001).

2. Brené Brown, *Daring Greatly: How the Courage to Be Vulnerable Transforms the Way We Live, Love, Parent, and Lead* (New York: Avery, 2012), 12. Brené Brown's books, as well as her TED Talks on the same subjects, have broadened my understanding of the significance of vulnerability. Also see Brené Brown, *The Gifts of Imperfection: Let Go of Who You Think You're Supposed to Be and Embrace Who You Are* (Center City, MN: Hazelden Publishing, 2010).

chapter 3

1. Andrew Murray, *Andrew Murray on Prayer,* (New Kensington, PA: Whitaker House, 1998). Also accessible online at www.world invisible.com/library/murray/praylife/prayer01.htm.

chapter 4

1. Bill Thrall, Bruce McNicol, and John Lynch, *TrueFaced: Trust God and Others with Who You Really Are* (Colorado Springs, CO: NavPress, 2004), 37.

2. Brené Brown, "The Power of Vulnerability," TED, June 2010, https://www.ted.com/talks/brene_brown_on_vulnerability.

3. Brené Brown, *The Gifts of Imperfection: Let Go of Who You Think You're Supposed to Be and Embrace Who You Are* (Center City, MN: Hazelden Publishing, 2010), xv.

4. C. S. Lewis, *Mere Christianity* (New York: HarperCollins, 2001), 218.

5. Robert Frost, *You Come Too: Favorite Poems for Young Readers* (New York: Henry Holt and Company, LLC, 1959), 84.

chapter 5

1. John of the Cross, "The Dark Night of the Soul," in Richard J. Foster and James Bryan Smith, ed., *Devotional Classics: Selected Readings for Individuals and Groups* (New York: HarperCollins, 2005), 33–37. These excerpts gave clarity to what God was doing in my spiritual journey.

2. Foster, *Devotional Classics*, 34.

3. Ibid., 36.

4. Ibid.

5. Ibid., 37.

6. Catherine Marshall, *The Helper* (Grand Rapids, MI: Chosen Books, 2001).

7. Catherine Marshall, *Beyond Ourselves* (New York: Avon Books, 1961).

8. Marshall, *The Helper*, 52–53.

9. Foster, Ibid., 37.

10. Foster, Ibid., 35.

11. Foster, Ibid., 36.

chapter 6

1. William Barclay, *The Daily Study Bible Series: The Gospel of Matthew*, vol. 2, (Philadelphia, PA: The Westminster Press, 1976), 15–16.

2. Ibid., 285.

3. Ibid.

4. William Barclay, *The Daily Study Bible Series: The Gospel of John*, vol. 2, (Philadelphia, PA: The Westminster Press, 1976), 8.

5. The term *redemptive remembering* comes from the following thoughts in the book *The Sacred Romance*: "Part of our journey forward is a journey backward into our stories, to bring all the events of our lives—the Arrows and the Haunting—into the light of the Sacred Romance for their proper interpretation." Brent Curtis and John Eldredge, *The Sacred Romance: Drawing Closer to the Heart of God* (Nashville, TN: Thomas Nelson Publishers, 1997), 205.

6. James R. Sherman, *Rejection* (Golden Valley, MN: Pathway Books, 1982), 45. More information on the quote available at http://quoteinvestigator.com/2015/11/05/new-ending/.

chapter 7

1. "Life Rhythm Theory," David Drury, last modified 2005, accessed May 18, 2017, http://www.drurywriting.com/david/05-LifeRhythmTheory.htm.

2. Ibid.

chapter 10
1. Sybil MacBeth, *Praying in Color: Drawing a New Path to God* (Brewster, MA: Paraclete Press, 2007).

chapter 11
1. Gary Thomas, *Sacred Pathways: Discover Your Soul's Path to God* (Grand Rapids, MI: Zondervan, 2000), 14. Thomas writes in his first chapter: "Over and over again we give Christians the same spiritual prescription: 'You want to grow as a Christian? All you have to do is develop a thirty- or sixty-minute quiet time and come to church every Sunday morning.'" If you're not familiar with this book, it's a helpful addition in understanding how you most sense God's presence in your life.

chapter 12
1. Keith Drury, *With Unveiled Faces: Experience Intimacy with God through Spiritual Disciplines* (Indianapolis, IN: Wesleyan Publishing House, 2005), 164.
2. Richard J. Foster, *Celebration of Discipline: The Path to Spiritual Growth* (New York: Harper and Row, 1988), 110.
3. M. Robert Mulholland Jr., *Invitation to a Journey: A Road Map for Spiritual Formation* (Downers Grove, IL: InterVarsity Press, 1993), 168.
4. Ibid., 159.
5. Dallas Willard, *The Spirit of the Disciplines: Understanding How God Changes Lives* (New York: Harper & Row, 1988), 138.
6. Ibid., 138.
7. Ibid., 137–138.
8. Ibid., 138.

chapter 13
1. Larry Osborne, *A Contrarian's Guide to Knowing God: Spirituality for the Rest of Us* (Colorado Springs: Multnomah Books, 2007), 135. This book has been reprinted as *Spirituality for the Rest of Us: A Down-to-Earth Guide to Knowing God*.
2. Drury, *With Unveiled Faces*, 7.
3. Keith Drury, *Spiritual Disciplines for Ordinary People* (Indianapolis, IN, Wesleyan Publishing House, 2004), 9.
4. Osborne, *Contrarian's Guide to Knowing God*, 182.